Your Most Enchanted Listener

Your Most
Enchanted Listener

WENDELL JOHNSON

International Society for General Semantics
San Francisco

For Edna—my favorite listener

International Society for General Semantics
San Francisco

Contents

Your Most Enchanted Listener

*All roads of wonder lead, with much meandering,
to the Rome of self-fulfillment,
a city within a city within a city without end.*

CHAPTER ONE

There Might Once Have Been a Wise Old Frenchman . . .

✳ There might once have been a wise old Frenchman who knew a most wonderful secret, which he longed to share with all who would but linger. To each of them he explained his secret with the patience and the vision of the olden prophets, and they, as one, exclaimed, "What rare poetic gifts you have!" The music of his words was to all of them enchanting, but the words of his music were as wind in the wheat.

The wonderful secret which the wise old Frenchman sought with unshrinking hope to share with all men, his brothers, was this: Only those who are wise to the words are the wise to whom words are sufficient.

With the concentration of a midwife he strove to make this plain to those who listened. With the gentleness of a new mother he abided their illusions of understanding by which they kept themselves from comprehending his profound though simple meaning.

Deeply he divined that, talking to themselves unceasingly, men spin without end a net of words by which their thoughts, indeed their destinies, are stayed. Men think with words, but seldom long about the words with which they think—like fish to whom the waters of the sea are incidental to the sea. Observing this, the wise old Frenchman was stilled by wonder.

Yet, there were the children, not yet numbed by learning. As he sat one day on a firm chair beneath a wide tree on his green yard, the wise old Frenchman beckoned to a boy who had come near.

"What would you call this?" he asked the boy.

"A hickory nut," the boy said.

"Ah, but I should rather call it a pon lomando, because it seems to me to be a much prettier name. Don't you think it is a much prettier name?"

"Much prettier," said the boy.

"Good! Then you and I shall call it a pon lomando," said the wise old Frenchman.

"I'd like that. Pretty names are much the best."

"You know what names are for, don't you, boy?"

"Of course I do," said the boy. "I use them for talking."

"Ah! They're good for that."

The boy laughed softly.

"And have you noticed how very difficult it is to make names without talking with them, at any rate to yourself?"

"Of course I have," said the boy.

"And making names is great fun, don't you think?"

"Nothing is more fun than that," the boy said. "I can make a name for anything."

"And change it any time you please?"

"Any time I please."

"Do you make new names because you grow tired of the old ones?"

"Sometimes I grow tired of the old ones," the boy said.

"Is it that you grow tired of them when they are no longer useful for making thoughts that are true or delightful? Then you make new names, do you?"

"I make new names then, because I like to make thoughts that are either true or delightful. They're the best," the boy said.

"Do you sometimes make two very different names for the same thing?"

"Of course not. It wouldn't stay the same if I made another very different name for it. Giving a thing a quite new name makes it be a new thing. Everyone knows that!"

"Oh, my boy, few men know that. Do you know what very nearly all men say? They say that a rose by any other name would smell the same."

"That's not true!" said the boy. "That's not true at all!"

"Of course it isn't true," said the wise old Frenchman. "I have made a verse about that, and you can learn it:

> A rose with onion for its name
> Might never, never smell the same—
> And canny is the nose that knows
> An onion that is called a rose.

The boy smiled quietly, and skipped away.

" . . . I like to make thoughts that are either true or delightful. They're the best," the boy said.

CHAPTER TWO

Four Hundred Little Tugs Each Day

✳ An ancient Chinese sage is said to have observed that it is easy to paint a goblin but hard to paint a horse.

It is hard to paint a horse, because ever since our first astonished view of one it has become more and more unlikely that there might again be a horse seen by us with eyes undimmed and undeceptive.

Just so, with each passing year it has become more difficult for us to recapture the first engulfing sense of "strange things happening" that we must have felt when first we spoke a word. As most of us toddled unsuspectingly into our second year of life, we still retained almost completely the enchanted point of view of the little child from Mars. So it was that when we found ourselves con-

7

trolling others from a distance by making noises in our throats, surely we were seized by what could only have been an unrelenting wish to make words and to watch their fantastic effects. At any rate, in the adroitly unpoetic wording of the academic experts, between the ages of one and three years the average child undergoes a language growth that he will never again equal in any later period of comparable extent.

Like March, speech comes in like a lion—a bounding and untiring lion—and goes out like a lamb—an unwell and monotonously bleating lamb.

If then we are to paint the horse of human speech, as it were, we must recapture a sense of wonderment concerning it. We may never hope to understand fully what we say so long as we think we already do. There is vastly more to the responses we make to and with symbols than we learned from our grammar books in school, or from our textbooks in college, whatever their drab titles might have been. Man is the animal that talks—if, talking, he is properly so called —and to try to understand him without understanding the difference that his talking makes is to come by the depraved conclusion that man is merely an animal. Yet an equally tragic outcome of our failure to grasp the difference that man's talking makes is seen in the undisciplined claim that it makes more of a difference than can be demonstrated. It is this that gives rise to the distracting view that men are hardly less than angels, and have no kinship with animals at all. To paint such a picture of human language and the difference that it makes is, indeed, to paint a goblin.

The key to an understanding of men, of course, is an appreciation of children, and children are never so enlightening as when, like mirrors of meaning, they reflect the coded hubbub by which they are surrounded. But this is something seldom well observed. We talk to children much as though to little manikins, and we miss so much of what they mean to say because we will not believe their speech is more than verbal friskiness. Meantime, wonder waits on the strangely unappreciated fact that the average four-year-old child asks four hundred questions a day! These hundreds of questions are like tiny ropes at which the child tugs unrestingly in the heroic effort to get the world inside his head. The fateful fact is that he does get the world inside his head—*a* world, that is. And it is the world in which he is to spend the rest of his life— unless he turns out to be one of those rare creative persons who retain a country boy's popeyed view of the common- place.

The kind of world a youngster gets inside his head may or may not be a good one in which to spend the rest of his life. At any rate, the kind it is, and is to be, depends on the questions the child asks and the answers his elders give him. It is largely their answers that he takes in and puts together to make his private world. It may be a dream world, a never-nowhere land. If it is, then the more he grows accustomed to it and learns to prefer it, the more bewildering for him will be the world outside his head. The person whose private notion of reality is out of accord with the world he finds by sight and sound and touch lives necessarily with uneasy feelings of confusion and insecurity. He bumps his shins where he had expected the soft flick of blossomed clover, and he moves warily, missing out on beautiful vistas, while he squints in search of dangers that are nowhere at all.

A child, of course, is much at the mercy of his parents

and teachers and the other persons who speak to him with tones of confidence and knowing. They even direct him in the questions he asks. They do this mainly by the answers they give—and fail to give. The answer a child gets to his first question limits, and determines, what his second question shall be, or whether there shall be one. In general, children are encouraged to ask those questions for which their parents have answers they want them to have. They are discouraged from asking questions for which the parents have no ready replies—or for which they have answers they do not want the children to know.

It is by such means that grownups determine, wittingly and unknowingly as well, the kind of world a youngster will get inside his tender head. If it is a world that does not correspond very closely to reality, the questions he goes on asking about it will have less and less to do with the hard, though useful, facts of daily living. And the answers he gets, while they may even come to be absolutely certain and unchanging in a wordy sort of way, will tell him little about the whats and hows of the world outside. In fact, the more such questions he asks, and the more such answers he receives, the more knowledge he gets that he can't use, and that other people don't agree with or care about. In plain words, he comes to know more and more, of no consequence, about less and less that matters.

If, on the other hand, the world a child gets inside his head represents fairly well the actuality surrounding him as he grows up, the questions he asks about it will have some bearing on the day-to-day business of living in the world of sights and sounds and fellow creatures. The answers he gets to such questions will seldom be certain and never complete, because they will be about the never-ending transition that we call reality—but precisely for this reason they will be useful. And the more such questions he asks, and the more such answers he gets, the more resourceful and serene he is likely to become. He is almost certain to learn more and more of what he needs to know in order to make fewer and fewer blunders, while worrying less and less about the things that either never happen or that happen in spite of anything anyone can do anyway.

Few things that even the most loving mother might ever teach her trusting child could hold for him a richer treasure than skill in asking questions and in judging the answers to them. It is a skill without which he will be fair game for intending deceivers, and the unsuspecting victim of well-meaning befoggers. Without it, indeed, he will be his own most misleading informer. With it, he will be able to help himself and others to make the most of such good will and good sense as may be abroad in this world where men abide so briefly. With it, in fact, he may learn to paint a horse— as well as goblins of enduring beauty.

Only those who are wise to the words are the wise to whom words are sufficient.

CHAPTER THREE

The Talking Tribes

✳ It is quite easy to tell our children from their pets. They use more lead pencils and make more sounds in their throats.

This is to suggest that man, like every other kind of creature, has specialized biologically in his own way. The beaver has gone in for strong teeth and a stout, flat tail. The rabbit has made the most of hind legs. Fishes have demonstrated what can be done with gills. The particular part of the body man has selected for purposes of working out his own distinctive kind of biological specialization is the brain, more particularly the topmost layers of the brain, the cerebral cortex.

The result of this has been something utterly new in the kingdom of living things. The animals have specialized in ways that have limited their possibilities of developing new forms of behavior. For example, once the rabbit managed to achieve the very wonderful hind legs which he now has, he was stuck with them; and he was stuck with the small number of specific things that can be done with such legs, chiefly some remarkable high jumping and broad jumping and a style of running that makes it possible for the rabbit to outspeed very nearly all comers. But just because the rabbit has equipped himself to do these things so very well, he has forever forfeited the possibility of being able to do certain other things in any fashion at all. Just so, once the rainbow trout had acquired that extraordinary mechanism called gills, it found that while it was able to live in water very well, it was also forever incapable of living out of water.

Man, however, hit upon a way to be fatefully different: he specialized in not specializing. It is the peculiar characteristic of the cortex of the brain that the thicker and the more wrinkled it becomes the more kinds of activity it makes possible and the more kinds of environment its possessor can turn to advantage. The result is that man, with the most luxuriant brain cortex so far achieved, is the most adaptable creature in all the world. He seems able to survive, at least for considerable periods of time, at practically any latitude, longitude, or altitude. Not only is he able to make out at the tops of mountains and at sea level as well, but he is also able to fly well beyond the mountain tops and to dive below the surface of the sea to impressive depths. The number of different ways in which a man can make a living is fantastically greater than the number of different ways in which the average squirrel or the typical codfish can provide for itself. There was once a persistent investigator who figured his way through a wearisome abundance of data to the conclusion that the average man can do at least 7,200 different jobs! Even the very most talented chimpanzee can lay claim to nothing like such flamboyant versatility. Man is, indeed, a specialist at not specializing. We are never so human as when we are effectively teachable and venturesome and, therefore, creatively adaptable.

All this is not to say by any means that man is, biologically speaking, a jack-of-all-trades and master of none. Because of his thickened and heavily wrinkled brain cortex, there is one particular thing he does better, much better, than any other creature, and in this respect he is a specialist in the usual sense of the term. He can create and use symbols so elaborately and with such effects as to make it impractical and misleading to classify man as an animal at all for many purposes.

As human beings we are a symbolizing class of life, and unless one wants to split hairs we are the only such class. An ancient man from Mars, familiar with the symbolizing equipment and activities of the most highly developed of our simian forebears, would hardly have predicted that in the course of evolution a creature would come along who would produce the *Oxford English Dictionary,* the custom of classroom lecturing and the comic strip. The difference between men and animals so far as symbolic behavior is concerned makes a critical difference. It is a difference in degree, if that be claimed, so great that it becomes absurd to insist that it is *merely* a difference in degree.

Symbolizing in the human being can, with advantage, be looked upon as a basic bodily process. At least one philosopher, Susanne Langer (*Philosophy in a New Key*), says in effect that it is of the nature of man that he must transform all his experience into words—or colored patches, melodies, bronze statues, or other patterns of symbols. He does this as naturally as he drinks water, eats berries, or makes love. Man, says Dr. Langer, has a basic need for using, for manipulating, arranging, recalling, inventing, changing, expressing and responding generally to and with symbols of various kinds. From this point of view, it makes no more sense to try to imagine ourselves never doing these things than it does to try to imagine salmon never swimming or wrens never nesting.

To wonder, then, why we talk to ourselves—as a rule, silently, of course—is much the same as to wonder why we sleep, or swallow, or scratch. We talk to ourselves, as a child would say, just because. Try looking at something—a lamp, ash tray, cup of coffee, anything at all—and see how long you can keep from saying words, making "inner speech," either about what you are looking at or about something else. Or, have someone near you snap his fingers three times during the next hour, and each time he does try to recall whether you were making "inner speech" just before he snapped his fingers. Or simply try to "make your mind blank" for even a few seconds. The process of symbolization rivals in its restlessness the other vital functions of the body. It is as though we move with pulsating verbal gills through a sea of words, ceaselessly extracting from it our food for thought.

It is vital that our wordways not be blocked. It is essential that we do enough talking and that we do it freely enough—to others, certainly, and to ourselves, too. It is not good for us to repress our thoughts or keep them to ourselves and to be tense wth pent-up feelings. There are few wisdoms more ancient than this—that talk, in appropriate doses, and under proper conditions, is a good and powerful medicine. Silent men are by no means always "strong." People who talk a very great deal may or may not be unserene; those who habitually talk very little are rather more likely to be, at least to some degree. The amount of speaking we do varies, of course, depending on circumstances, levels of fatigue, interest, and need, but there is a roughly definable average amount of speaking that we accept as normal. We tend to take special notice of people who "don't talk enough" or who "talk too much."

There are, of course, other important aspects of normal speech behavior. One has to do with what is talked about, especially the degree to which we talk about ourselves, our intimate feelings, particularly our bothersome feelings, our personal problems. We do not insist that anyone bare his soul to all the world, but we rather assume that any normal individual will now and then talk freely to someone, one or a few close friends, perhaps, wife, husband, lover, and, when advisable, a professional listener, such as a lawyer, minister, or psychological counselor. People differ tremendously meanwhile in their readiness to "strip down" verbally, to throw off the superficial layers of polite small talk and reveal their private feelings. On the one hand, it tends to be true of individuals who "talk too much" that they conceal their inner selves behind the verbal smoke screens they create, chattering along about big issues or spouting inconsequential chitchat as though they were compulsively running away from the things that matter most to them. People who "don't talk enough" are, on the other hand, less elaborate about it. It isn't so much that they try to run away verbally from topics of conversation that would be painful to them; rather, they stay very still, hoping the danger will go away, that the others will go on by with the conversation and not notice them.

A third facet of normal speech behavior is reflected in the mood or attitude, the evaluative tone, in which the talking is done. Voices affect us as ranging from pleasant to unpleasant, from cheerful to depressed, from friendly to hostile. And not only do voices vary in such ways, but so also do the words used, the accompanying gestures and facial expressions. We recognize this in the common wisdom that, within rather broad limits, it isn't what one says that matters so much as how one says it. We recognize a generally normal mode of speaking, or at least we are struck by what we take to be the inappropriate, the offensive, and the insincere. To the people who talk to us we respond more or less positively, more or less negatively, according to the evaluative tones of their speech.

Nor is this all, of course. We also expect normal speech to be clear enough to be understood reasonably well and with reasonable ease. First of all, we ask that it be clear as to enunciation, not mushed or mumbled. It is not that we are intolerant of the differences that make for individuality in appealing and constructive ways. We are positively attracted by regional and national differences among speakers—dialects, we call them. A dialect can add to the charm of a coed from Georgia, and it can add to the income of a physician from Vienna. But however distinctive or strange speech may seem we do prefer that it be intelligible. As Bing Crosby discovered, to his fortune, we like to recognize the words.

And we like to know what the words mean. We expect normal speech to be clear in this sense, too—plain, that is, comprehensible. We enjoy vaudeville double talk, of course, and we appreciate the fact that a specialist has to use an occasional term that is new to us. In fact, we do not object to technical books that are completely beyond us, or to taking courses of training in order to learn how to read them. What we do object to is unnecessary gobbledegook, Federalese, legalese, and the doctor who says rhinitis when he means a runny nose—unless he's speaking to another doctor, to whom he can Latinize to his professional heart's content for all we mean to do about it. Our only point is that when he, or anyone else, tells us something, we want to feel reasonably sure we know what is being said to us about what. And if we think it might not be entirely or necessarily true we like to be clear as to just what we are doubtful about.

Finally, to complete a list that is practical rather than exhaustive, we expect normal speech to be dependable, provided it is supposed to be informative or factual. If it seems untrue we want its meaning to be clear enough, as we have suggested, for us to be fairly sure about how to check up on its truth or falsity—but we really prefer that it be true as well as clear. There is something profoundly unfortunate, we feel, about a person who lies much, and the best thing we can say about anyone who frequently gives us misleading information because of honest bad judgment is that he is a nuisance. Whenever speech is supposed to be informative in a factual sense, we ask that it be made up of clear statements and true ones, so far as that is possible.

What we generally recognize, then, as normal is speech that is appropriately frank and personal, expressive of a mood proper to the occasion, and that adds up to "about the right amount" of talking under the circumstances. In addition, we expect it to be sufficiently clear to be understood without undue difficulty—clear, that is, as to enunciation and clear with respect to meaning. If, moreover, it is supposed to be informative, we expect it to be reasonably dependable, or true.

It is of particular importance that we talk with others sufficiently. If we are to realize abundantly the wonderful human difference that it makes to us to be able to use symbols, especially the symbols of our common speech, we must use them enough—and we must use enough of them—to achieve the values to be gained from them.

Man's store of legends and folk wisdom records in lavish detail the practices and the benefits of meditation, confession, and free discussion. We know, as though by instinct, that it is good to "pour out our sorrows," to "confess our fears," to "talk things out." The democratic process itself is, at bottom, a system of government by common speech, reflecting a profoundly felt and cherished need for free expression. All our great religions betray the deep hunger we feel for meditation and confession.

We are the talking tribes. The tongue is the most mobile structure of the human body, and to fetter its symbolic gestures is to dry up the deep springs of our human-ness.

These are sentiments which abound not only in the counsel of wise teachers and physicians, but also in the better wisdom of the common people of long ago and of today as well. To be human is to speak. To be abundantly human is to speak freely and fully. The converse of this is a profound truth, also: that the good listener is the best physician for those who are ill in thought and feeling.

And these truths stand out most sharply when applied to that strangest of all spectacles to be seen in the realm of living things: a man talking to himself—like wind carried on the wind, like water borne by water. A man is never so serene as when he hears himself out, granting to himself the quieting freedom to speak fully without fear of self-reproach. Nor is he ever so gravely ill as when he stops his tongue with crying out "Shame! Shame!" unto himself. The thoughts that we forbid ourselves to whisper and the feelings that we will not say we know are the measure of our self-abandonment. By stopping up our own ears against the sounds of our own voices we achieve not the peace of inner stillness, but the unnerving disquietude of haunted consciousness.

The realization toward which we are beckoned by these reflections is that if we are to become as fully human as we might we must not only talk freely to ourselves, but we must wholly listen too. For if we will, it will occur to us to question what we say—to ask ourselves what we most deeply mean by what we tell ourselves, and how we know that what we say is true. And if we then insist on answers we can trust we shall grow wise in finding them.

*. . . talking to themselves unceasingly,
men spin without end a net of words
by which their thoughts, indeed their
destinies, are stayed.*

CHAPTER FOUR

The Early Morning of the Human Day

✳ If we would understand a man by his words it is best that we listen to what he says when he is either in trouble or in love. For if we do, and if we are quiet and attentive, we will notice that no matter how fully he may be taken over by the illusion that it is to us he speaks, he talks at such times most surely to himself.

Pondering this, we come in time to realize that every speaker is his own most captive listener. And as we grasp the meaning of this more and more firmly, we are appalled by it. Because now we see something that had quite escaped our notice before. We had not often thought of speakers as their own listeners, and so we had not attended to them in a spirit of eavesdropping, as though listening in while they were talking to themselves. And now, in the spirit of eavesdropping, we can hardly help noticing that people talking about themselves and their private desperations are saying the most fantastic things to us, to themselves, that is. They are saying so much that is just not true, and much that is questionable at best, and they are saying it all as though it were to be taken for granted as wholly true, listening all the while quite unwonderingly to themselves saying these things. What is even more distressing, there is such a great deal that they might be saying to themselves that would be true and liberating, and we wait for them to say it, but they so seldom do, at least not in any very clear and self-informing fashion. So it is that, listening to themselves, there is so much they rarely hear that they should be hearing over and over again.

Watching all this going on in front of us, there are things we call to mind. Blind men, for example. A blind man, we realize, has no way of knowing what precisely there is about a sunset that he doesn't see. We wonder whether he can even know that he is not seeing a sunset. Indeed, it would seem that a blind person who has never known what seeing itself is like could hardly know at all that he does not see—or, at least what he would understand by this must necessarily be quite different from what we who can see would understand by it.

And so we think of blind men and sunsets as we sit listening to people talking—to themselves—about their troubles, wondering whether they could possibly know what they are not saying, whether they could even be aware of the fact that they are not saying it. Listening, we can find no way to believe that they understand the difference it would make to them if they knew not only what they do not know but also that they do not know it.

Observing more closely—which means, most particularly with fewer preconceptions—we begin to see that what is still more important is the fact that they do not even realize that they are talking to themselves, that they are being affected by their own words. Most people, most of us, appear to believe that we shouldn't talk to ourselves, so far are we from knowing that we do in fact talk to ourselves—not usually aloud, of course—unceasingly and unavoidably all day long. And if we thought we did talk to ourselves we wouldn't admit that we do, so far are we from understanding that most of what we experience as thinking, wondering, "making up our minds," regretting, or longing, or being contented is a kind of talking we do to ourselves every day from morning till night—and on through the night in the free movies inside our heads that we call our dreams.

Pursuing such reflections, we come at last to feel strangely dumbfounded. Can it really be true, this deep unawareness that we seem to have of the unceasing symbolic processes inside our own heads? This great never-lifting mist of unconsciousness through which we appear to move so unsteadily—can this be real?

And can it be, as it surely seems, that this all-engulfing gray mist of unperceptiveness through which we grope is inhabited—is haunted? It appears to be haunted indeed, not only by the disembodied evil spirits and gods of our own unremembered creation, but also by the disfigurements of our fellows which we abundantly fashion from our private misunderstandings and discontents. It is haunted, as well, and thickly, by grotesque reflections of ourselves, as though we were moving through a shadowy hall of mirrors that we do not remember having entered and from which it does not occur to us to seek an exit.

Certainly all this is not something that we are able to capture, if only briefly, and to contemplate with wonder, and then fling carelessly away upon the unreturning wind. Above all, we feel driven to make quite sure that what we seem to see and hear is not, after all, illusion. For, certainly, if it is not illusion this can only mean that men—we, that is—are still wandering about in the early morning of the human day.

We have only begun to notice where we are and what we are about. What thinking we have done certainly has not been concerned primarily with ourselves. Most of us, if we can be honest, will admit that we have done precious little thinking of any systematic sort about the deeper reasons for our conduct and particularly about the process of thinking itself, especially our own. We have, however, done some thinking of other kinds—and it has been quite effective and suggests that we do have promising ability—we have done some thinking about such things as oil, coal, metals and the like. We have learned to process natural materials in most impressive ways, and even to create synthetic substances that nature forgot to contrive. We have made wheels and levers, invented engines, learned to fly, and put together enormous factories turning out products made wonderful by the amazing principle of interchangeable parts. We can send a message around the world before we can finish a sneeze. We are by no means stupid. In many ways we have shown that we are incomparably more clever than even the shrewdest primate or the most meticulous wasp.

It is our very cleverness, however, that we understand so dimly. The individuals among us who have been the most clever—the Galileos, Shakespeares, Einsteins—we don't pretend to understand very well. We say they are geniuses, which is a way of shrugging our shoulders, of saying nothing except something like, "It is His will," or, in common slang, "Search me!" So we express our feelings, wanting explanation. So far from understanding our "geniuses" we sometimes become greatly afraid and distrustful of them. We have killed a few, tortured many, and inconvenienced nearly all of them.

With respect to the dangers of man's destructiveness, it is later than we think—because with respect to the cultivation of man's constructive and co-operative tendencies, it is far earlier than most of us imagine. It is so early that there are men still living who were children when the world's first laboratory for the scientific study of human behavior was established by Wilhelm Wundt at Leipzig, Germany, in 1879. And this was a very small laboratory. Even so, with few exceptions, there was nothing like it in the United States until the present century. The first institute in America devoted to the scientific investigation of normal children, the Child Welfare Research Station at Iowa City, was not established until 1916.

It seems likely that few of today's leaders in government and public affairs in this and other countries have more than a freshman-course knowledge of the science of human behavior and its imperfections. And these imperfections are all too often those from which, in various forms and degrees, they themselves suffer—with consequences from which we all suffer. Moreover, most commentators and historians seem not to be properly trained to note or evaluate this crucial circumstance.

Surely no other single fact could have more important effects in relation to public affairs, and so ultimately in relation to our private affairs. Listening to men of state talking about the national and world problems confronting them, we cannot help recalling ordinary people talking about their own personal problems. There are in some measure the same indications that the speakers are naïve with respect to the psychological and symbolic—and so the human—factors involved in the problems they are talking about. There is also a similar tendency to speak with a firmer tone of finality than the speakers' apparent knowledge and comprehension would appear to warrant. There is the same failure, more often than we would wish, to ask the needed questions and to say the more constructive things that might be said, and the same apparent lack of awareness of all that is not being said. And there is a like tendency for the speakers not to realize clearly that they are their own most affected listeners.

We think of blind men and sunsets.

We need greatly, as surely we all appreciate, to have in high places men capable of speaking to themselves in public with wholesome effects on themselves and on the people who listen to them. We need leaders who realize, at the very least, that they are in fact talking to themselves as well as to others, and who are disposed to listen thoughtfully to their own voices with the welfare of all their other listeners constantly in mind. In the meantime we can protect ourselves against either cultivated or witless persuasiveness, most especially our own, only if we are trained to listen alertly, not only to others but to ourselves as well. Sound is so much with us that we perform the wonder of listening with very nearly the innocence of the beasties afield. We listen, save in our keener moments, as artlessly as we breathe. But, while under practically all circumstances Nature and the medulla oblongata will attend to our breathing for us, we can entrust our listening to our reflexes only at the risk of losing our birthrights.

The art of talking to ourselves is an auditory art as much as it is a vocal one. Its cultivation requires us to listen well through all the hours of day upon day to what we tell ourselves as we give the only answers we can fashion to the questions we are driven to design.

We ask ourselves. . . . We say unto ourselves. . . . And, listening in, we come, if we are watchful and reflective, to know shade by shade, though never wholly, the persons we have been and are and are becoming.

*We may never hope to understand
fully what we say so long as we
think we already do.*

CHAPTER FIVE

The Wanted Wise Man

✳ The truly great teachings that have deepened and enriched man's humanity have been few, and slow to be learned. Confucius taught his fellows the wisdom of caring for their families. A thoughtful carpenter of Galilee fostered the deeper wisdom of caring for all mankind. These two have been among our greatest instructors in the ways of good will.

Aristotle trained his pupils to be logical, to reason, to draw necessary conclusions from stated premises. Two thousand years later Galileo fashioned the even more important art of drawing from observation and from experience generally the sorts of premises from which only reasonably sound conclusions might logically be deduced—for further checking. These two have been among our most revered teachers in the ways of clear thinking.

31

Good will without clear thinking can be monstrous: men of all lands have always marched behind the bright banners of righteousness as they have gone forth to do the killing they glorify as war, and always they have come home from battle to benedictions. Clear thinking without good will can be fully as lamentable: millions of human beings have been reduced to wasting torment by their shrewder fellows. Mankind needs desperately one more great teacher—the wanted wise man—who will bring about a close union of clear thinking and good will.

If such a teacher has already appeared we shall hardly be sure of it until his instructions have had more time to affect us. There is meanwhile a possibility, not impatiently to be dismissed, that we have entered upon the Year One of a new era. If we have, it is an era that will surely be defined by the consequences of applying the *methods* of Aristotle and Galileo to the *problems* of Christ and Confucius. It will be defined, that is, by the effects of applying scientific method—which includes reason—to problems of value and good will. And in this epochal undertaking, the basic and indispensable art will surely be that of asking questions. It is an art that men everywhere will need to make as much a part of their lives as slowly through the centuries they have in some degree made loyalty, love, logic and respect for facts common denominators of their professed ways of living.

One can hardly help seeming presumptuous in making statements such as these. One runs the risk, as well, of appearing simple-minded. To summarize the course of the human pageant to date by implying that men—or significant numbers of them, at least—have learned to have fair feelings about one another, and to make clear and honest statements where their feelings are not deeply involved, is to make a generalization almost too broad to accept with confidence. And to go on from this to say that what men need most to learn, in addition, is the art of asking questions, is to seem to underrate the problems men face. After this has been said and pondered, however, one may gain a sustaining reassurance from the simple fact that the art of asking questions has been fantastically undervalued when it has been recognized at all.

It is not an art that is wholly new. Even before Galileo the techniques of inquiry were not entirely undeveloped, and with Galileo certainly, some three hundred fifty years ago, the basic rules of factual investigation became quite clear. But they were known to very few at that time, and these few had no way of foreseeing the world-changing implications of what they knew. They were far more impressed —and today still men are more impressed—by the *results* of factual investigation, or scientific labors, than by the *method* used to bring about the results. Men, except the very wise and ingenious, have always valued answers more than questions. And so, for the most part, we have overlooked the tremendous importance of the sorts of questions that are essential in the solving of our problems. We can appreciate such questions and their utterly basic significance only as we see and understand the part they play in the method of discovery which Galileo thrust upon us, and which we have used since to transform so strangely a world our forebears so innocently took for granted.

We may gain a general sense of the part played by questions in the method of science by looking briefly at the method as a whole. Stripped of its elaborate technicalities, unusual vocabularies, and strange machines, the method used by scientists is essentially the same regardless of their special fields, and it appears to be very simple. It involves four steps:

Question
Observation
Report
Conclusion

And these four steps recur over and over again, new conclusions generating new questions, and new questions leading to new observations, and still newer conclusions, newer questions, et cetera, endlessly.

The man who works at being a scientist is, first of all and above all, a man. Outside his laboratory he eats, sleeps, shaves, mows his lawn and goes to ball games, spoils his children and boasts to his wife, as other men do. And while he shaves, or turns restlessly upon his bed, he thinks, worries, and wonders. He is preoccupied. Occasionally he "gets" an idea. Usually it "comes to him" in the form of a doubt or a guess. When he gets back to his laboratory he refines it: he makes it into a question. And this question is especially designed to lead him to make certain observations. These observations will be the ones he needs in order to confirm or refute the doubt or the guess with which he started. But, of course, he must report his observations accurately, rather than wishfully. And he must reason clearly from the factual report to a defensible conclusion—a generalization, hypothesis, explanation, or prediction. And by his conclusion he is not allowed to rest; it stirs in him the vague tensions of new hunches and curiosities, and leads him to new questions and so to further observations, and on and on as in a great unending spiral of supposing and supposing and supposing.

These, then, are the things a man does when he works at

being a scientist. He may do them with a staff of technicians and millions of dollars worth of apparatus—or he may do them all by himself with a piece of string. The millions of dollars and the piece of string are incidental. What is essential is that he have a reasonably dependable nervous system and a habit of following the rules of the game he is playing.

The major questions that scientists ask themselves, as factual investigators, are of two kinds:

1. What is it? How does it look and smell and taste, what does it sound like, and how does it feel?

2. How does it vary with what?

The answers they get to these two kinds of questions make up the only two kinds of substantial knowledge we ever have about anything. That is, we can know what something is like to an observer—how to recognize it, describe it, and how to define the words we use to describe it; we can know how it differs from other things; we can classify it in various ways. And we can know how it behaves, how it waxes and wanes, grows, changes and decays, under what specific conditions. That is, we can know how it varies in relation to other things. In other words, what we call our knowledge consists, on verbal levels, of (a) definitions and descriptions and (b) statements of relationships among the things we know how to describe with the words we know how to define.

This is all quite general, and a few examples should help to make it somewhat more clear. Consider any disease; cancer, for instance. When we say we do not understand cancer very well we mean that although we can recognize it, see it and describe it, we do not know much about the particular conditions under which it comes into being, develops, and disappears. In practical terms, then, we appear to know fairly well what it is, but we know much less evidently about the possible ways of preventing and combating it. The main question we have yet to answer regarding cancer is: "How does it vary with what?"

Stuttering (perhaps you call it stammering) is another good example. We are coming to understand stuttering reasonably well, although until quite recently it was generally regarded as one of mankind's most mysterious afflictions. When we say we are coming to understand it reasonably well we mean that we can describe it clearly enough to tell the difference for practical purposes between it and other forms of behavior that resemble it—such as normal non-fluency, neurotic blocking, or impaired speech due to brain damage or paralysis. We mean, also, that we know something about the home and school policies and practices that tend to make children stutter. We know something about the conditions under which stuttering gets worse and better. And, since we know something about the conditions under which a stutterer's speech improves, we know, to that extent, how to treat it. There is need for further research, a great deal of further research, but we have managed to build up useful answers, though partial ones, to both questions: What is stuttering? How does it vary with what? And to the degree that we have, we can say that we now have some understanding of stuttering.

Suppose we look briefly at one other example, one that has long been and still is a vast and perplexing problem: war. No one, it appears, may claim to know the answers, in any decisive breadth or detail, concerning the problem of war. Here, for the most part, is a situation in regard to which it may sensibly be said that a fool is one who knows nothing but answers—and the wise man is one who knows what the questions are. We need to work at asking the needed questions about war, and to be less influenced by those who are convinced they already know all the answers.

One of the more forthright and hopeful answers so far advanced is that of Dr. Brock Chisholm, Canadian psychiatrist. Dr. Chisholm raises some doubts about our habit of taking profoundly for granted that the effects of our local moralities are good. The doubts he raises come close, in fact, to being positive statements about the warlike consequences of these local, provincial moralities. Dr. Chisholm asks what factors in our culture could be responsible for our engaging in systematic campaigns of murder approximately once every generation, and the answer he gives is sobering:

What basic psychological distortion can be found in every civilization of which we know anything? It must be a force which discourages the ability to see and acknowledge patent facts, which prevents the rational use of intelligence, which teaches or encourages the ability to dissociate and to believe contrary to and in spite of clear evidence, which produces inferiority, guilt and fear, which makes controlling other people's personal behavior emotionally necessary, which encourages prejudice and the inability to see, understand and sympathize with other people's points of view. Is there any force so potent and so pervasive that it can do all these things in all civilizations? There is—just one. The only lowest common denominator of all civilizations and the only psychological force capable of producing these perversions is morality, the concept of right and wrong, the poison long ago described and warned against as "the fruit of the tree of the knowledge of good and evil. . . ."

Misguided by authoritarian dogma, bound by exclusive faith, stunted by inculcated loyalty, torn by frantic heresy, bedevilled by insistent schism, drugged by ecstatic experience, confused by conflicting certainty, bewildered by invented mystery, and

loaded down by the weight of guilt and fear engendered by its
own original promises, the unfortunate human race, deprived
by these incubi of its only defences and its only reasons for
striving, its reasoning power and its natural capacity to enjoy
the satisfaction of its natural urges, struggles along under its
ghastly self-imposed burden. The results, the inevitable results,
are frustration, inferiority, neurosis, and inability to enjoy
living, to reason clearly or to make a world fit to live in. . . .

Let us go back to Strecker and Appel's definition of maturity
[in *Psychiatry in Modern Warfare*]. "The ability to size things
up, make one's own decisions, is a characteristic of maturity."
"A mature person . . . has the qualities of adaptability and com-
promise." Were you and I brought up in that direction? No; we
were taught to be absolutely loyal and obedient to the local concept of virtue whatever that happened to be. We were taught
that Moslems or Hindus or Jews, or Democrats or Republicans
(with us in Canada, Grits or Tories) or capitalists or trade
unionists, or socialists or communists, or Roman Catholics or
Methodists or any of all other human groups are wrong or even
wicked. It almost always happened that among all the people in
the world only our own parents, and perhaps a few people they
selected, were right about everything. We could refuse to
accept their rightness only at the price of a load of guilt and
fear, and peril to our immortal souls. This training has been
practically universal in the human race. . . .

"The mature person is flexible, can defer to time, persons,
and circumstances. He can show tolerance, he can be patient,
and above all he has the qualities of adaptability and com-
promise," say Strecker and Appel. . . . Helping their children
to reach this state of maturity successfully is the first responsi-
bility of each generation. Only when this has been done successfully can we hope to have enough people able to see and
think clearly and freely enough to be able to prevent the race
going on as we have gone, from slaughter to bigger and better
slaughter.

Other men have expressed other provocative views. Many —particularly many psychologists, anthropologists, and other scientific investigators of human behavior—agree more or less with Dr. Chisholm. But even if we grant that they are right, we cannot grant that their answers are wholly clear and exhaustive in a course-of-action sense, nor would they seem to claim this, however important they, and we, might feel their views to be. As yet, as we all must realize, we do not know what all the detailed questions might be that would lead us to make the further observations from which we might gain a fully operative understanding of war, one that could lead to an effective program of prevention. We do know what the big general questions are. There are two of them: (1) What is war or peace? Just what would be a relatively useful description of the thinking and behavior, individually and socially, that make up what we call war, on the one hand, and peace on the other? (It might well be, of course, that the most important aspects of the problem are to be found in the semantic no man's land that lies between "war" and "peace.") (2) Precisely what conditions—economic, moral, political, educational—bring about, or increase, diminish, or eliminate warlike behavior or relationships? These two general questions would seem to define the problem and set the task we have to undertake if we are ever to achieve an understanding of war that will enable us to abandon it.

So far, most of us, and most of our leaders, in all countries, have hardly begun to ask these questions. Peoples throughout the world are still largely in the relatively provincial and compulsive name-calling and self-justifying stage, the primitive stage of unreflective self-righteousness and single-minded devotion to their respective local loyalties. Our

understanding of war is so meager that we seem incapable
of grasping how meager it is. We have, for the most part,
not even begun to think about war; we simply prepare for
it and engage in it about once every generation—not counting "cold" wars and "skirmishes." And only during fairly
clear periods of truce, if ever, may most peoples clear-
headedly and safely wonder aloud why this is so. We still
have to take—or at least largely to complete—the first step
in a scientific approach to the problem, that of asking the
questions.

What we have come to call the sciences are simply those
fields of endeavor in which men have learned to ask more
or less clearly the two kinds of questions we have been discussing. The workers in physics and chemistry, for example,
devote nearly all of their attention to finding out how substances and processes might be more precisely and discrimi-
natingly and usefully described, and how they are function-
ally related. The result is that practically any physicist,
while he may or may not be a boring dinner guest and woe-
fully uninformed about politics or modern art, almost always
talks sense where his own work is concerned. In his work-
shop he daily achieves man's greatest measure of freedom
from superstition and poppycock.

In those fields of endeavor that we think of as not being
scientific, there is rather more concern with purely verbal
definitions than with factual descriptions. There is more
care given to reasoning logically—or merely with deep feeling—from vague or questionable premises than to making
the premises themselves clear and defensible. Where functional relationships among facts are not compulsively ignored, they tend to be treated casually, naïvely, and vaguely.
The questions usually asked in these non-scientific fields

are not easy to answer, when they can be answered at all in any sensible fashion.

Outside these "fields" lies the vast and inescapable domain of daily life. It is a fairly new idea, entertained as yet by a rather small number of adventurous souls, that one might behave scientifically in this domain. This seems preposterous—until one comes to grips with the strangely enlightening question of just how one might go about it to behave unscientifically in any situation. Just exactly what would one have to do to avoid being scientific at all? Evidently, as a minimal requirement, one would have to ask no clear questions, avoid looking fully or steadily upon what there is to see relevant to one's beliefs, give misleading accounts of such observations as one might make, and traffic in false or delusional conclusions about one's experiences. There is something at least slightly unnerving in the realization that probably the best place to go in order to find behavior such as this is a hospital for the mentally disordered.

If these remarks arouse any curiosity about the differences between scientific and unscientific behavior, we are ready to examine with some care the matter of how to ask a question. For if there is any one thing that most sharply distinguishes scientific behavior, whether in the laboratory or the living room, it is the kind of questions it involves. And the most sharply distinguishing feature of these questions is that they are the kind that can be answered directly or indirectly by means of factual information that can be obtained, now or conceivably in the future, or that has been obtained, by making observations.

Let us consider, then, how to ask questions that can be answered in a factual sense, in order that in some modest measure we might avoid wasting our lives in "unraveling the webs that have never been spun."

*The wise man knows what the
questions are.*

CHAPTER SIX

The Ordeal of Asking Questions

✳ "How much snush is there in ten tons of slerv?"

The lesson to be learned by staring at this "question" for a few moments is simple but fundamental: it is that the first principle of befuddlement lies in using words unclearly.

This being true, it follows that the surest way to get a clear answer is to ask a clear question. Only a fool who needs a psychiatrist—and possibly the psychiatrist he needs—could tell us what "snush" or "slerv" might mean in the above question. If for you these "words" are simply blanks, that is a good sign. If, on the other hand, you seriously wonder how much snush there really is in ten tons of slerv, your nearest of kin should be notified at once.

All this is, of course, too obvious to labor. One might not

be quite as certain, however, as to what would be a sensible reaction to such a question as this: "What is the unpardonable sin?"

For most people it is quite likely that this question would create far more confusion than the previous one. The "snush" question would usually have little, if any, effect; it would simply be dismissed as silly. This question as to what is the unpardonable sin, however, is more likely to be taken seriously. It seems to be about something real. It contains only standard English words, commonly used. It has a question mark at the end. It looks very much like hundreds of other questions that people ask—and seem to answer—every day. Most people might not feel sure they know the answer to it, but many would. Very few would doubt for a moment that there is a correct answer to the question, if only the man who knows it or the book that contains it might be found. It would be a rare and very wise person who would ask, "What does the question mean on the level of not-words, the level of observation and experience? That is, precisely what factual observations might I or anyone else make in order to answer it?"

If there be abroad in the land the one more great teacher mankind so desperately needs, surely he is telling us, among much else, that if the one who asks a question cannot indicate at least roughly how the factual observations needed to answer it are to be made, he has asked no question at all. He has only made sounds in his throat. They may be, of course, sounds of arresting quality, expressive of profound feeling, whether of joy or torment. We may be strongly moved by them, and respond with sounds equally dramatic. For the human signs of gladness or despondency do most certainly affect us—and among the most engrossing of these signs are the "questions" men ask with a wild light, or with tears, in their eyes:

"Hast thou seen God! With thine own eyes hast thou seen Him!"

"Do you truly love me! More than anything else in all the world!"

"Why, oh my God, why did this have to happen to me!" And these, you see, are exclamations. They are not questions. And we may not answer them in the confident tones of certain knowing without acquiring the attitudes of fraud.

We may answer *to* them, of course, with exclamations of our own—or with the steadying monotones and chants of ritual, or with fervent or reassuring caresses. We may answer to them as we would to the crying of a wandered child, or to the rapture of a new mother overwhelmed by the warmth of her baby's breath.

Life without exclamations would be, surely, oppressively less than human. Not only as individuals, but also as whole societies, we give way to exclamations—not only to tears and laughter all our own, but also to Thanksgiving Day and Christmas, Bastille Day and Yom Kippur, Labor Day and New Year's Eve. And by these all our years are gladdened and enriched.

When, however, it is information that we seek and explanations that we desire, the sighs and shouts that punctuate our search are hardly responsible for our discoveries —any more than Archimedes' shouting of "Eureka!" was the means to the great insight that prompted it. If we would build a bridge or catch a mouse we have need of dependable observations, and we must ask the questions that direct us to them. It is part of our folk wisdom that we realize this, and so we have learned to build bridges quite well and to catch mice when we put our minds to it.

If we have not learned to build so well the structure of a personality, or of a social group, or to catch so adroitly the elusive facts that comprise exciting peace, we had best look, first of all, to the questions we ask—and fail to ask—as we fumble our way, for all we know, all together and each in his own curious fashion, to the refuge of the psychopathic ward and the unnerving shelter of the lead-lined cave.

The art of asking questions—the art without which clear thinking and good will may never quite be joined—is to be come by only through discipline beyond that to which we are accustomed. Moreover, it enforces changes in our personalities and ways of life which most of us have never dreamed of undergoing. A staggering price is demanded: in order to ask the questions that might bring better answers than those we already have we must be prepared to cast aside the answers we have, the very answers indeed that we have learned to trust because they were given to us by our parents and our moral exemplars and our teachers.

This means that in order to gain a saner world we must abandon the world we know. We must give up those things that make our lives distinctively different from what they could more fruitfully become. Among these things to be abandoned throughout the world is each man's fearfully trained readiness to defend unto death and without question his own particular local beliefs, customs, institutions and ways of thinking, whenever they come into grave conflict with the equally local and particular beliefs, customs, institutions and ways of thinking of others who are equally ready to defend them unto just as dead a death and as completely without question. Meanwhile, only at the risk of survival, clearly, may we abandon our defensiveness while yet we have need of defenses. And only at a cost in vigilance may we question our need for vigilance while need for it exists. The dangers we know we may not wand away merely by wishing that we might cease to create them. And they block the road to what we might have been. The road is tortuous and long, and the green valley to which it winds is not to be reached "without question."

Ultimately and as a prerequisite to the brave new world, if such there is to be, question we must. And most difficult and essential of all is the questioning of humanity's failures to question. What we take for granted is especially to be re-examined with the uncompromising honesty of scientific inquiry. For it is in precisely those regions of our thinking which we—which people everywhere—have most stoutly protected from rigorous investigation, where we have insisted science does not apply, that we seem most likely to discover our delusions and the sources of our conflicts. And rigorous investigation, here as elsewhere, necessarily begins by refashioning or abandoning all those questions that are not to be answered sooner or later by the observations that we can make and trustworthily report.

This is a price for clear thinking that is to nearly all of us alarming, and few men, even among those of the greatest good will, have ever been prompted or willing to pay it. It is difficult, of course, to accept the fact that the ordeal of asking clear questions is so severely taxing, and that the clear thinking that they alone make possible demands such a shocking sacrifice of our accustomed self-defensiveness. It is a sacrifice that we can want to make only after we have gained depths of maturity yet rarely visited. But having plumbed these depths, doubtless we shall find sacrifice transformed into privilege, and gladly we shall trade our tarnished yesterdays for brighter new tomorrows.

And if we then insist on answers
we can trust we shall grow wise
in finding them.

CHAPTER SEVEN

Seeing What Stares Us in the Face

✳ The story has been told of how a
professor came to be dismissed from the faculty of a university during the Middle Ages: in the course of prolonged
dispute concerning the number of teeth there are in a horse's
mouth, he brought in a horse!

The hero of this forlorn footnote to human history sym-
bolizes both the basic method of genius and the hazards of
its use.

The hazards vary, of course, with one's circumstances—
and prudence—but the method does not lend itself to com-
promise. It is, as we have seen, a method that involves four
steps—question, observation, report, conclusion—and they
are to be performed in that order, and over and over again.
Without questions that require observations, and throw a

49

steady beam into the places where they might be under-taken, either no observations will be made or, if they are, nothing will be made of them. And as soon as clear questions have been asked, we have no choice but to set about making the observations they require—except as we may cherish our ignorance and conspire with ourselves to preserve it.

The alternatives to asking answerable questions, and then making honest attempts to find answers to them, are clear—and disgraceful. We can ask no questions at all, either out of stupor or as as a display of arrogance. We can ask questions that are misleading, or vague, or meaningless—to be answered, respectively, by mountebanks, the confused, and the very naïve. Or, we may ask clear questions and then refuse to acknowledge them, as a gesture of fear, smugness, or irresponsibility.

The one form of human behavior that is consistently honest by conscious design is that behavior which is scientific. If you really believe that honesty is the best policy then you will strive to behave as scientifically as possible. If you try it you may decide against it, but then at least you will know that, by so far, you prefer dishonesty. In that case you are likely to be comforted by the arguments advanced by Mr. Stefansson in favor of "the standardization of error" (in an unforgettable book by that title) on the ground that generally agreed-upon error would be—that it is, in fact—more convenient than truth. For one thing, truth tends to change as the restless atoms weave anew and anew the shimmery fabric of fact. Error, on the other hand, agreed upon and firmly fixed in legend and in law, is something one can count upon from day to day, even from century to century.

And there are other considerations. Truth peeks from

behind the most unlikely hedges at the most embarrassing moments. It discredits the old—to the corrupting delight of the young. It tarnishes brass hats and soils vestments. Error, standardized and sanctified, is, by contrast, discreet and reassuring. It gilds our incompetence with the arresting luster of honor. It gives to our accepted foolishness the iridescent glow of wisdom, and in a thousand other ways as well confirms our benevolent conviction that we are wiser than we seem. If these you take to be advantages then all is clear.

If, however, you feel compelled to reject these appeals to the comfort and convenience of deceit, you will be relieved to find a method for the madness of your honesty. We have examined the first requisite of the method: the fashioning of questions that can be answered by means of observations that can be made. It is time now we considered the honest ways of making these observations.

The most important thing to know about an observation is that it has to be made more than once, by more than one person, before it can be entered with confidence in the ledger of fact. Truth is never private.

These, of course, are fighting words. Few other pages of history are so smudged with blood as those on which the masses of men have written—and are writing—their determined declaration of independence from those presumptuous few who claim to know by secret revelation what is best for them. This was the basic issue of the French Revolution—and the American Declaration of Independence. It has ever been the argument, punctuated by gunfire, against the Kings. It is the sword that hangs heavy over the head of every dictator—military, political, industrial, academic, religious, legal, familial, or of any other stripe. It is the justification of democracy.

Science and democracy acknowledge no Stone Tablets, no Sons of Heaven, no Führers, no Medicine Men or Shamans. The truth does indeed make men free—free from the tyranny of Knowers—for there is no truth except as it has been confirmed by those for whom it is intended. In the economical phrase of Carl Sandburg, "The people, yes."

Precisely because an observation is the act of an individual, there is no way of knowing whether it is true—dependable, that is—until at least one other individual has made it, too. And this holds regardless of who makes it first. The first beholder may be a potentate wound round with gold braid, fastened together with medals made from silver soaked in milk drawn from the seventh cow sired by the seventh bull, and blessed by the incantations of seven aged men who never face anywhere but east. It makes no difference. Somebody has to agree with him closely enough to make the observation reliable for practical purposes. The more other persons there are who agree with him, and the more closely they agree, the better. And it doesn't matter who they are so long as they are independent and properly equipped, trained, and situated to see what he said he saw. If they see it, too, he can be believed accordingly. If they don't, the chances are he is a fraud, and any person of usable wit will hold in reserve this possibility until further notice.

This is the sort of thing scientific workers refer to when they speak about the reliability of their data. They are talking about the limits within which two or more observers, with comparable opportunities for seeing the same thing, agree in what they see. The greater the agreement among qualified observers, working independently of one another, the more reliable the observations they report. This concern for observational agreement is such a fundamental preoccupation of scientists that a large share of their labors goes into the job of devising methods for insuring that their observations, upon which their knowledge and theory depend, shall be as reliable as possible.

In the laboratory this makes for a tremendous amount of work and ingenious invention—and for more and more dependable findings. Outside the laboratory, in the ordinary circumstances of everyday life, it makes for a habit of mind conducive to rigorous honesty and integrity. In the absence of this habit of mind injustices and tragedies of bias tend to be widespread and inevitable. For reliability, in the fundamental scientific sense, is essential to fair play. It is presumed as a prerequisite of democratic legal procedure. This is an issue, therefore, that has tremendous personal and social consequences outside laboratories as well as inside them. The rules of honesty, as they apply to observational reliability, cannot, with honesty, be set aside sometimes. They pass, as it were, through any and all walls, those of marble and mud alike.

In the names of justice, good sportsmanship, and general honesty, it is simply essential that information reported in the public press, in meetings of committees, or across lunch tables be double-checked. In engineering and industry this is a matter of profits or bankruptcy. In medicine it is a matter of life or death. In public affairs and in private life it is a matter of integrity or corruption. In the laboratory it is taken for granted as a necessary and elementary part of scientific behavior.

If you would be reliable, dependable, honest, you may not report as an established fact whatever has not been observed by more than one person—even though you be that one person. And those who verify the observation must be suitably equipped and situated and sufficiently unaffected by suggestion, illusion, or self-interest.

Facts are public, and he who buys a secret gives alms to fraud.

All this is said, of course, with the clear realization that facts arise in experience—and every experience is personal. It is necessarily, in each instance, the experience of some one individual. An act of observation is no exception to this rule. In the case of an observation made by you of something outside your skin, I can verify it. But if you say you feel a pain in your back I cannot feel it too. How, then, am I to establish reliably that you do feel a pain in your back? You may be lying, or malingering, or you may need a psychiatrist.

The fact is that I may not fully verify your reported feeling by myself. For it must be checked by observations of its circumstances and effects, and my own observations of these circumstances and effects are to be checked by at least a second observer, independent and competent. Assuming that they are checked and found to be reliable, these observations are the evidence by which your report is to be judged. It may not be conclusive evidence, but it is the only evidence we can have, and quite often—as in medical practice—it will be dependable enough to be useful. Certainly, if no evidence can be found of any physical reason why there should be a pain in your back, it is to be concluded that probably either you are giving a false report or you are neurotic. And there are observational checks for determining which is more probably the case. If you are neurotic you do have a pain in your back—because of an idea in your head—and proper procedures, observational again, will be more or less likely to reveal what the idea is, and how it can be altered to get rid of the pain.

So it is that even our reports of the observations we make of the goings-on and feelings inside us are to be judged as being more or less reliable, depending on the relevant additional observations that support them or not. To insist, "It's my back and I ought to know," does not in the least degree convince a scientist.

The basic rules of observational reliability are simple, however widely untaught and unlearned they may seem to be. As a matter of fact, we trust them constantly, in certain respects, even though it may not often occur to us that they are the rules we are trusting. We know from common experience, if not from controlled experiment, that as a rule the readings of thermometers, meters, scales, and the like are reasonably reliable, and so we tend to rely generally on our own thermometer readings and observations of speedometers. Whenever we have checked them against the readings made by our companions they have turned out to show considerable agreement and so to be fairly dependable, as a rule. Having established the practical reliability of a particular kind of observation as commonly made, we live with it—at tolerable risk. So it is that, without bothering to check every report by which we are guided, we manage to survive in large numbers, in spite of depths of innocence that are essentially beyond sounding.

Facts—reliable observations—are worth no more to us, however, than our points of view and our philosophies permit us to make of them. There is a kind of fruitless cunning in much of our surviving—a reliance on facts that are, in truth, dependable for purposes of taking breath, together with an equal faith, all too often, in the lies and nonsense that forever frustrate our reachings out for love and peace and wisdom.

Yet, the facts of observation are indispensable to our sanity, and they can and do affect our points of view, our basic attitudes and philosophies. Certainly there is no way for us to look upon the truth, and align our living with it, except as we may learn to see what stares us in the face. For, seeing not what we look at, we see what is not there at all. And holding fast to visions, we consume our lives in fitful struggle with devils of our own invention, encouraged and commanded by the angels that we dream.

It is by learning to see what stares us in the face that we may triumph over self-deception, since it is a kind of learning that depends upon our trusting the testimony of our fellows to challenge and complement our own. For there is a trickery about our senses that makes our seeing all suspect, save as we test it for the stray effects of fancy. And only far more testing than we mostly think to do can make it fancy-free.

*There is a trickery about our senses
that makes our seeing all suspect.*

CHAPTER EIGHT

The Believing That Is Seeing

✳ There was an old codger who said, "Believe in baptism? Of course. I've seen it done."

The seeing that is believing and the believing that is seeing make of the world we make for ourselves a haunted habitation. We are remarkably adept at believing what we have never seen—and at seeing what we have come to believe.

This we may understand so far as we understand projection. Projection is a bodily process. It is part and parcel of the workings of the nervous system. Most of us know far less about it, however, and are much less directly aware of it than we are of our other bodily processes, such as digestion and breathing. Even those who know little about their own digestive functions are at least made keenly aware of them now and then by the wordless eloquence of pain or

59

comfort. But the workings of projection are all but concealed from our inlets to direct awareness. We learn of our own projections, when we do, mainly through circumstantial evidence.

This circumstantial evidence arises chiefly in connection with certain of our mistakes in perception and judgment. They are the kinds of mistakes, in many cases, that we can make over and over again without suspecting that we are making any mistakes at all. In fact, in some of their forms, they are mistakes that we simply must make if we are to go on believing, feeling, and behaving as we have been trained and encouraged to do by our unrelenting teachers, love and fear. And by the same token they are precisely the mistakes that we must cease to make if we are to achieve the changes that we prize as self-development.

The basic fact about projection is simply this: *What we look at is not what we see.*

What we see is determined not alone by what stares us in the face, but also by our wishes and our doubts, our likes and dislikes, our fears, assumptions, knowledge, and ignorance. In general, it is what we take for granted, our fixed beliefs and settled expectations, that we project outward, coloring and distorting—even obliterating or creating—whatever there may be in our field of stimulation. It has been summed up in pat fashion by Ralph Evans, color-control expert, in *The Scientific American* (August, 1949, page 55): "We see what we believe we are looking at. Our mental pictures are our own. They are not necessarily shared either by others or by the objects themselves." And sometimes we see what isn't there at all: the believing that is seeing.

Except as we understand the process of projection we can

neither trust our own observations nor evaluate properly the reports made to us by other observers. When we tell ourselves what we have seen—or heard, touched, tasted, smelled, or felt—our words refer in some measure to something other than what they seem to be about. When we say, "It's hot in here," we seem to be talking about the temperature of the room; more directly, of course, we are reporting a bodily state. A fever perhaps. The remark is largely about us, and may say little that is trustworthy about the room.

There are other examples of projection that are more important by far than this one, of course. When we tell ourselves—and others who may be listening—that Mr. Jones is queer, we may do more harm than we could achieve by outright physical assault, unless we and all the others concerned realize that the statement is not about Mr. Jones in any descriptive sense. It represents a projection of our own tastes, standards, feelings and knowledge, or lack of understanding. It is chiefly a statement about ourselves.

The process of projection can be illustrated by means of the simple diagram in Figure 1.

The most sobering thing to note about the process diagrammed is that a great deal happens between any event in the outside world and any statement we may make about it. This means that there is some measure of self-projection involved in anything we say. That is, it is unavoidably true that regardless of what else we seem to be talking about, we always in some degree are talking about ourselves.

It is at Stage 5 in Figure 1 that we represent the words we tell ourselves—or others. We usually take for granted that these words are about reality—the events at Stage 1, the sources of sensory stimulation in "the world outside." But Stages 2, 3 and 4 are passed through between Stage 1 and

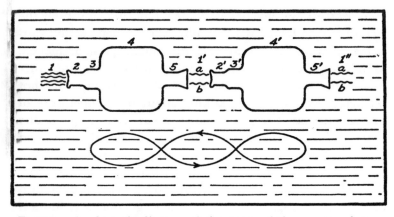

Figure 1. A schematic diagram of the stages of the process of communication. When Mr. A talks to Mr. B (and Mr. A and Mr. B may or may not be one and the same person, of course) these things happen at the various stages: at (1) an event occurs which at (2) stimulates Mr. A through his eyes, ears, or other sensory organs. The resulting nerve impulses travel to Mr. A's brain, affecting whatever may be going on there to produce at (3) a pre-verbal state of affairs. It is this state of affairs that Mr. A, at (4), begins to transform into words, according to his available verbal patterns, and out of all the statements he might possibly make he selects, or abstracts, at (5), only certain ones. These he utters and they become, at (1′), light waves (a) and sound waves (b), by which, at (2′), the eyes and ears of Mr. B are stimulated—and everything that happened to Mr. A at Stages 2, 3, 4 and 5 now happens to Mr. B at Stages 2′, 3′, 4′ and 5′. It doesn't stop there, however, since either Mr. A or someone else, or Mr. B himself, responds to Mr. B's spoken words, and, as the arrowed loop in the diagram indicates, there are interactions (spiraling, or ever-changing, rather than circular, or repeating) among the various stages so that, in a sense, everything is affected by everything else. Adapted, by permission, from previous diagrams by the author in "The Spoken Word and the Great Unsaid," *Quarterly Journal of Speech,* Volume 32, December, 1951, published by the Speech Association of America, and *People in Quandaries: the Semantics of Personal Adjustment,* published by Harper and Row, Publishers, New York, 1946.

Stage 5, and what goes on at these stages goes on inside our own skins. What we say at Stage 5, therefore, is necessarily about ourselves as well as something else, at Stage 1, that we take to be reality. In fact, our words may, and often do, say nothing at all about reality (Stage 1). They can be, and often are, expressive only of our inner states—feelings, preconceptions, assumptions, delusions, or hopes. It turns out sometimes, because of this, that what we report to ourselves —or others—as factual observations are mainly or purely self-projections.

The chain reaction that leads to this fateful outcome can best be understood if we trace it backward from Stage 1. What occurs at Stage 1 seems strange almost beyond belief. The wavy lines in the diagram at this point represent what passes between Mr. A, the speaker, and the somewhat more mysterious character, Mr. B, the listener. What passes from Mr. A to Mr. B are sound waves and, in face-to-face situations, light waves. Occasionally, in addition, Mr. A may tug at Mr. B's coat lapels, pat his shoulder, or in other ways attempt to inject his meanings into him by hand, so to speak. But if we disregard for the moment the semantics of caresses and blows, we may cover the main essentials by limiting our attention to sound waves and light waves.

The light waves reflected by Mr. A are recognized by Mr. B as facial expressions, smiles, frowns, or as gestures, postures, bodily movements, etc. And, truly, "every little movement has a meaning all its own." Moreover, we depend heavily on the meanings the movements seem to have as we try to interpret what a speaker says. Even when we cannot see the speaker we visualize him. That is why we are so often surprised when we meet for the first time someone whose voice we have heard. Having projected our own conception of how a man with such a voice should look, and having taken our projection for granted, we are astonished by the man's actual appearance. Thus, we make countless mis-evaluations of what speakers say to us, not only by paying undue attention to their appearance, but also by giving too much weight to our sheer fancy concerning what they look like. It is indeed a wonder that we understand one another as well as we do—and we do not, of course, understand one another as well as we usually think we do.

The sound waves produced by Mr. A are interpreted by Mr. B as words and intonations. The same words can mean more or less, or their meaning can vary from black to white, depending on how they are spoken—or received. The mood and purpose, and the previous life history, of the speaker—and of the listener—are the living context which determines what the words shall mean and what effects they shall have. You will find the more substantial meaning of a word in the speaker's past love affairs, or present thyroid gland—or the listener's aching head, perhaps—rather than in anybody's dictionary.

There is a particular art, the art of persuasion, that has as its major purpose the control of the effects that words shall have. It is among the oldest of the arts, and one of the first that each new human being seeks, unconsciously, to cultivate. It is one of the extremely practical arts, and as such it can be as detrimental to our best interests as it can be essential to our welfare. Its consequences depend upon the skill and the purposes of those who practice it. The professed masters of the art publicly proclaim their good intentions. Those whom I have known personally, incidentally, make up an impressively ethical and conscientious group. Their ideal, they make clear, is the good man speaking well. All men know surely, however, that it is far easier to recognize an apt speaker than a good man. What is more important, there appears to be no necessary or even close relationship between the effectiveness of a man's speech and the goodness of his purposes and effects. The persuasiveness of Hitler was, in the minds of most observers who were not his followers, equaled only by the evil of his designs.

In all this the most significant consideration would seem to be that in school and out we place far more value on being persuasive than we do on being intelligently evaluative of persuasiveness. It has frequently been demonstrated that listeners are definitely influenced by such things as the manner in which a speaker is introduced, for example, and by what the listeners interpret as his likableness and physical attractiveness. In a Northwestern University study by Franklyn Haiman, as reported in *Speech Monographs* (Vol. XVI, No. 2, 1949), these factors were found to count more than did "competence," as rated. Such findings suggest with alarming emphasis that the art of listening is probably the most neglected of all those arts that might have, if cultivated, immense survival value.

As one consequence of this neglect of listening, and of the other forms of evaluative reaction, we are a society fantastically devoted to wrappings. Never mind the contents. At least, contents equal, we tend to go for the more eye-wooing container. Equal amounts of equally good bath powder, for example, can be purchased at prices ranging roughly from twenty-five cents to ten dollars, and amazing numbers of us pay up to $9.75 for precisely nothing but a small colored box and, of course, the incredible feeling of superiority that goes with taking sole possession of such a jimcrack. What comes in bath-powder boxes, however, is not extremely important.

It is what comes wrapped in bright banners or in mink coats that we need to know how to take or leave alone.

Almost the hardest lesson for the members of the symbol-using human family to learn is that there is no necessary relationship between the truth—or the value—of words and the manner in which they are expressed. Wisdom can be spoken as well by the homely and tattered as by the handsome and smartly uniformed. Truth can be scrawled on the back of an old laundry slip as well as it can be printed in many colors on heavy slick paper. It can be stuttered or lisped ungrammatically with a nasal twang as well as it can be uttered in flawlessly fluent rich tones precisely articulated. It is not to be lightly considered that a speaker may have trained his voice for forty years, and still use it to express sheer nonsense.

The sound waves and light waves that pass from Mr. A to Mr. B are in and of themselves without meaning. Their significance is to be found in the responses made to them. When these responses are made by Mr. B, the listener, they can be readily observed wtihin practical limits. The spreaders of propaganda—advertisers and special pleaders generally—are well aware of this, and go to considerable trouble to examine the responses they bring about, whether in the form of voting, buying, applauding, attacking, or joining. We are usually far less attentive, however, to what goes on when the responses made to Mr. A, the speaker, are made by Mr. A himself, as his own listener. Yet it is the responses we make as our own listeners that are undoubtedly the most fateful of all. For every speaker—to say it again—is his own most affected eavesdropper, and that is why the art of talking to ourselves is one that we may not neglect save at the ever-present risk of growing self-distortion.

We started out by saying that it is at Stage 5 (in Figure 1) that we represent the words we tell ourselves and others. What we find at Stage 1 are the forms that verbal expression (or any other kind of symbolic expression) takes in passing from Mr. A to Mr. B. Now, what we observe at Stage 1 is to be understood with reference to Stage 5—and what occurs at Stage 5 is to be understood by examining Stage 4, which precedes it, and so on back through Stages 3, 2 and 1. We need, then, to know what occurs at each of these stages in order to interpret with any competence the events at Stage 1 by which we are directly stimulated as listeners. And so we shall examine, during the next several chapters, the essential processes and the possible disorders at each of the stages indicated.

First, however, there are a few more general comments to be made. One of these is that what goes on at Stage 5 amounts only to a kind of final selection of the words we actually speak. These words are essentially a final draft of the preliminary attempts and revisions carried on at Stage 4. What occurs at Stage 4 may be viewed as the beginnings of the process of symbolization, in many ways the most curious process in the whole of our bodily economy. It involves the dumbfounding transformation of plainly non-verbal physiological goings-on into words and other symbols. Because it happens we are human. To most of us it is a sheer mystery, and no one understands it except in a most meager fashion.

One thing seems quite clear, however: *all we can ever transform into symbols is some bodily state or other of our very own.*

At one instant there is going on within our nervous system a silent and wholly non-verbal process; in the next instant this changes into a pattern of nerve currents, "mental pictures," "thoughts," muscle movements, and sounds—and we call this pattern speech. We say we talk facts, but it is certainly not highways, locomotives, and apple pies that, as magicians, we turn into the words we speak. It is, instead, our own bodily processes, inside our own skins, that we transform into the words we breathe into the windy code of speech. We say we talk about facts, but between the facts, the events at Stage 1, and the words we form at Stage 4 and utter at Stage 5, a great deal transpires. And it all transpires right in our own insides. The facts in the world outside are strained or filtered through our eyes and nerves and brain, and there is a resulting state of affairs inside the nervous system. It is this internal state of affairs, not the facts outside the nervous system, that we directly symbolize. In this sense, and it is an elaborately disregarded and extremely significant sense, *we always necessarily talk about ourselves.*

It is by no means easy to make clear to ourselves just what does occur when nervous impulses flip our tongues about so that we sculpture our breath into the evanescent forms of speech. But this much appears undeniable: the words formed at Stage 4 represent, stand for, are transformations of, and so are directly and immediately about, the bodily events at Stage 3 rather than the events outside the body at Stage 1. There seems no escaping this utterly crucial fact. The implications of this generally unnoticed but fateful happening are meanwhile far-reaching and gravely challenging to many of our most thoroughly accepted beliefs. The serious examination of it and its many meanings requires, conspicuously, an exceptional capacity for acknowledging our accustomed delusions and errors, wherever encountered, and for adapting to the disquieting adventure of new insights.

Practically all of us have been trained, for example, to

regard certain truths as self-evident, certain teachings as inspired, certain persons—and books—as infallible. This means that we have been trained as though there were—at least in the infallible persons and the writers of the infallible books—no merely human processes sandwiched between Stage 1 and Stage 5. We have been influenced—by well-meaning persons who in nearly every instance loved us very much—to be uninformed about, or to disregard, the plain fact that even the most respected authority is, after all, a human being. Between the words he utters and the world he utters them about there are physiological goings-on inside him, even as there are in you and in me—goings-on as glandular, as neural, and individualized as those that intercede between our own perceptions and our own reports of them. This is not to say that all men are equally fallible, that one man's opinion is as good as another's. It is to say that no human being is infallible. No one is or ever has been free from self-projection. No one, no matter what his title, age, attire, or name, or the veneration of the balcony from which he speaks, utters truth unfiltered and unaffected by his own protoplasmic tissues—and so by the patternings of his own peculiar background of experience and rumination. There is no one whose words we may accept without scrutiny, whose evaluations we may responsibly decline to evaluate. So far as we may determine, there are no books not to be questioned, no men who know for sure.

This is a stark, and for many perhaps a gravely confounding, way of indicating what is meant by the innocent-appearing fact: between Stages 1 and 5 of the communication process lie Stages 2, 3, and 4.

It will not be said too often if it is said again: what goes on inside the body at Stages 2, 3 and 4 is by no means a duplicate of the events outside the body at Stage 1. Moreover, all that happens inside the body limits and goes far to fashion the statements that are made at Stage 5. This is what is meant, fundamentally, by projection. And it is, of course, self-projection. It is a bodily process, as natural and as unavoidable as any other bodily process. We cannot eliminate it. We can only be more or less aware of it, and more or less honest and adept at taking it into account when we evaluate what we say—to ourselves as well as to each other. And we can be more or less forthright in warning our listeners that the statements we make to them are, in fact, self-projections. Our listeners are to be clearly and often reminded that we cannot utter, that no one can utter, factual truths that are absolute, unstrained by human protoplasm.

Unless we are aware of projection, seeing does become believing and believing seeing. One who is unconscious of projection can be persuaded—can indeed hardly avoid persuading himself—that nothing is something and something is nothing. Such a one is not only inclined to encourage himself to pursue mirages and to frighten himself with his own bemused interpretations of the moonbeams on his bedroom wall. He is also likely to take as his leader anyone properly behatted, and he is even capable, if he has the talent, of becoming himself a leader, taken in as completely by his own exhortations and official postures as he would be by those of any other rightly besymboled authority. Benito Mussolini was once appraised in such terms by Frank Heller, the Swedish novelist (in *Twilight of the Gladiators,* translated by Llewellyn Jones, Putnam, 1944): "If he did not become great it was because he let himself be drugged by a poison which is more dangerous than opium or hashish— by words. He talked so much and so often that at length he took his own words for reality and lost contact with the world."

Such a destiny is common for men whose tones are sonorous. And for all of us, sonorous or no, the worlds we manage to get inside our heads are mostly worlds of words, words that become our unrelenting own. And so it is that in these worlds of words inside our heads we hold ourselves captive. To a far greater degree than we are prompted to suppose we do, we take our words to be reality, and by so much we lose contact with the world outside the bony brain cases from which we peer nearly unsightfully.

We differ most wonderfully from all unspeaking creatures when we are conscious of words and what we do with them and because of them—and what they do to us—and when we are aware of our bodily processes of perception and symbolization, of projection and abstraction. The magic of symbolic communication transforms men into humanity. And so in the pages now to be turned we shall try, stage by stage, to become as conscious as we might of the wonders there are in the wonder of symbolization.

What we look at is not what we see.

CHAPTER NINE

Certain Fundamentals of Nonsense

✳ One of the most tantalizing truths we know is that there is so much we may never know. Because we can perceive so well the limits of our ability to perceive at all, we know that the most distant regions of our ignorance are destined to remain forever unexplored. We simply cannot overtake the coy horizons of the sea of unawareness that surrounds our modest island of perception. On this fact rests securely the conviction that humility is a vital part of wisdom.

The basic fact to be considered in this connection is that the eyes, ears and other sense organs of the human body are impressively limited in their capacities to respond to stimuli. They are, so to speak, tiny, dusty windows that let in but little of the light of the world. The wave lengths we recognize as light and color are but a small portion of those known plainly and deviously to the physical sciences. The vibrations we register as sound are but a fraction of the full range of air wave frequencies. We smell faintly and erratically, and at the extremes of the narrow range of temperatures to which we are sensitive we quickly die either by freezing or shriveling. Our capacity to discriminate by taste is so slight as to be utterly demoralizing to any but the most tolerant or disillusioned of chefs. And individual peculiarities in these respects are dumbfounding: there are persons who cannot smell a frightened skunk, and others to whom vanilla tastes like strawberries. And all this, of course, is in addition to the fact that a considerable proportion of the human family is either blind or deaf, or nearly so, and large numbers of the rest of us have at least minor sensory impairments. It is as though we were living all our days inside the sealed control room of a spaceship, with vague vibrations from somewhere outside beating faintly and fitfully against our frail antennae.

Moreover, together with the meager direct information we receive from the outside world, we are able to gain through our internal senses only a skimpy set of signals from the complex and continuous events inside our skins. Indeed, we hardly know at any moment what is going on either around us or inside us. The world as we see it, smell it, or sense it in any other way is certainly a patchy picture of the world we would perceive were we equipped with sensory organs responsive to the full range of energy manifestations. Moreover, what little we can sense would appear quite different if only our perceptive apparatus were not so compulsively subject to the laws of illusion.

True, we have indirect inferential knowledge of sorts

concerning those portions of energy spectra that we cannot directly sense. We have even learned to make use of many of the unsensed wave frequencies in the operation of radios and other instruments that contribute to our world of sound and sight, or that affect our bodily processes, as in the case of X rays and radioactive isotopes. But to the extent that we take the "naked-eye world" to be reality, we obtain a picture so limited as to be necessarily distorted and untrustworthy. Talking about what we can hear, see, and feel is a far cry from talking about the reality that is independent of our sensory soundings of it.

As a matter of fact, we do not talk much about what we hear, see, or otherwise sense directly. The native Zulu does not see the ghosts he talks about. Nor does the nuclear physicist see the electrons and neutrons about which he speaks. The clergyman has never laid eyes upon the heaven he describes, and no mother has ever directly sensed the "human nature" with which she accounts for the deplorable, or pleasing, behavior of her children.

Even when we do mean to speak about the world as we observe it, we talk largely in terms of our feelings about it or our judgments of it. We do not often *describe* things, persons, and events; we more commonly *evaluate* them as beautiful or good, wise or stupid, ugly or bad. Such words, of course, describe nothing. They express our personal standards and reflect our feelings about whatever we may be responding to.

Not only, then, are we greatly limited in our physical capacity to sense directly the world surrounding us—and the goings-on inside of us—but we also tend to disregard much of what we can, or could, sense. The worlds of words and pictures inside our heads, which we almost always take seriously and to which we feel a nearly deaf and blind loyalty, can hardly be anything other than a mixture of fact and fancy—and we can seldom be quite sure which is which. Moreover, we usually take the "truth" of them so wholly for granted that we rarely wonder, if we ever do, whether they might be misleading and just how they might be made more sane and dependable. As a rule, we speak of the worlds inside our heads with proud confidence that we are talking about the world that is outside.

And we act accordingly. We develop traditions and customs, pass laws, build institutions, formulate foreign policies and personal ways of life based on our largely unexamined mental patchworks. In doing all this we actually create a kind of social reality—a world of stone and steel, national boundaries, international treaties, laws and social customs—which amounts to a great collective self-projection, in which, as it has been said, there is nothing natural about 99 per cent of the things we do. It is a kind of ersatz world in which there is a convincing plausibility about our old codger of a few pages back who said, "Believe in baptism? Of course. I've seen it done."

A tremendous number of the things we believe in, because we see them done, are done for no other reason except that we believe in them.

It is one of the more curious aspects of all this that, in such a human-made world, common sense involves the delicate art of being just unsane enough to be practical. That is to say, what most clinical psychologists call social adjustment lies in part in the fundamentally negative skill of not making oneself too conspicuous. Good adjustment for any individual, therefore, is generally assumed by these clinical workers to depend more or less on his feeling, thinking, acting pretty much as other people do, of liking what they like, hating what they hate, believing what they believe—and not knowing why. From this point of view, the acquiring of new knowledge and skills, and a heightened consciousness of abstracting and symbolizing, can be hazardous. It is, in fact, one of the serious risks of education that it tends frequently to alienate the child from his parents, to make it more and more difficult for him to feel at home at home.

To parents as well as teachers, generally speaking, the good child is the one who agrees with them readily and shows no bothersome inclinations to go poking around among the possibilities of making life over into new and unfamiliar designs. Most of us appear to be psychologically discomforted, at least slightly, by appeals from those bent on enlisting us in their missions of social reform. We feel vaguely that slum dwelling, for example, is in some ways more normal than the dissatisfactions its effects arouse in compassionate welfare workers. Even war is evidently widely thought to be more natural than the feeling that it is undesirable. Peace on earth is an ideal to which we contribute generous ceremonial tribute, though not without uneasiness over its disquieting promise of no more fighting.

The process of communication, discussed in the preceding chapter, is to be understood in the light of considerations such as these. Stage 1 of this process, as diagramed in Figure 1, involves events external to our sensory end organs, whether these end organs be located on the body surface or in the lining of the stomach. These events are necessarily what we talk about, however indirectly, to the extent that we talk sense. To say that we talk sense is to say simply that what we talk about has been or can be *sensed,* or that our statements can be reduced to references to something that is sensible or perceptible, and that we can determine by means of sensory impressions whether our statements are reasonably true or dependable. Even what we say about electrons (which no one has ever seen) can be utilized or understood only to the degree that it can be interpreted by meter readings, photographs of deflected light beams, and other *sensible* things, which we interpret as though there were electrons, and as though electrons behaved as we quite arbitrarily assume they do.

The only possible check we have on our projections is that afforded by our sensory experience. It seems hard to believe that anyone should need to be reminded of this three hundred and fifty years after Galileo, but anyone who can read the newspapers or understand a word that he hears knows, of course, that three hundred and fifty years have not been enough for the clear teachings of the father of scientific method to take significant effect in the thinking of most of us. We still accept, celebrate, and honor a tremendous amount of sheer verbal assertion, particularly when it is presented by appropriately draped authorities to the accompaniment of music, banners, and symbolic gestures to which our responses of deference have been thoroughly conditioned.

To say that we speak nonsense—non-sense, that is—is to say that our statements do not refer directly to anything we can sense, and that they cannot be checked indirectly by reference to our sensory experience. Such statements, then, are essentially words gone whimsical. As such, they may be regarded as poetry or fiction and, so regarded, they can afford us deep pleasure or inspire us to grand sentiments. Taken at their face value, however, as though they were factual, they can only lead to a more or less elaborate out-of-touchness with reality.

It is possible, of course, to become quite precise in gauging the degree to which what we say is about what we sense. We can examine the nouns, verbs, adverbs and adjectives contained in our statements, and arrive at a practical estimate of the extent to which they are specific and clear in what they refer to that can be seen, heard, or otherwise sensed. Whole sentences, or phrases, or thought units can be evaluated in this way, as well as single words. Moreover, it is possible to measure one's vocabulary for any particular kind of sensory experience: one's vocabulary for representing colors, for example, or sounds, odors, tastes, and pressures. Ralph Evans (*Scientific American*, August, 1949, page 52) has made this observation: "In the 500 most frequently used words in the English language, according to the Thorndike-Lorge word counts, there are only 15 related to vision in any way. Of these only five are concerned directly with color. These are the words 'color,' 'light,' 'white,' 'green' and 'red.' "

It is feasible to measure an individual's ability to describe differences between any two things—a peanut, say, and an oyster—with respect to size, shape, appearance, the sounds that can be produced by means of them, odor, taste, texture, weight or heft. Sensory discrimination, whether demonstrated by what one says or by what one does in response to pairs or patterns of stimuli, represents one of the psychologist's more important fields of scientific investigation. The methods, facts, principles and laws in this field are presented in almost every elementary psychology textbook. It is possible, as such available knowledge makes clear, to be quite precise in describing the responses made by an individual to the events occurring at Stage 1 of the process diagramed in the last chapter.

The more we know about these events at Stage 1 the better we can understand the behavior that we show in response to them. But there is something impractical to the point of absurdity in the view that every man in the street should be as fully informed as a specialist concerning such matters. In the meantime the very least that anyone needs to know in order to insure his own sanity reasonably well is that it is possible—it is, in fact, easy and it is common—to talk nonsense. It is possible and it is ordinary to see what one believes only because one believes it, and to believe in a seriously misleading fashion what one sees. Moreover, it is impossible to sense directly more of the world about one, or of the processes inside oneself, than the sensory receptors with which we happen to be born are able to respond to. A tremendous share of our knowledge, therefore, must be gained by inference. But our inferences can all too readily run wild except as they are adequately checked against what we can sense.

We have learned to be on guard against those who, as we say with naïve glibness, cannot tell right from wrong. We have far more to be concerned about, however, in the person who cannot tell a fact from a phony. For such a person— especially if he feels sure that he does know right from wrong—is likely to be a bigot, a tyrant in his own grand or petty fashion, or at the very least a benign misinformer and a public nuisance. And the very worst that might be so is that this could be true, even if only seldom and slightly, of thee and me.

It is possible and it is common to see what one believes only because one believes it.

CHAPTER TEN

Before Words

✳ Once the tiny, dusty windows of our senses have let in a little of the light of the world, it undergoes a strange transformation. What had been light waves become what we speak of—as though we knew that we were talking about—as nerve impulses. Racing along the sensory nerves, these impulses arrive quickly in the cell tissues of the central nervous system. They pass, as best we can infer, through a series of relay stations, from the sensory end organs to the spinal, thalamic, and cortical levels, and then along outgoing nerves to the muscles and glands where they bring about contraction and secretion. These activities give rise to additional nerve currents which travel back into the central nervous system, and out again to the muscles and glands, and so round and round. It all adds up to a sort of circulating, or spiraling, or reverberating "feed-back-and-forth" process that is continuously affected by its own effects.

Johnson's First Law, which is that one thing leads to another, and which is seldom if ever found to be undependable, is probably never more abundantly verified than in this unending chain of stimulus-response-stimulus-response which makes our lives more and more complex and complicating, mystifying and meaningful, from before the dawn of birth to the moment when the lights of life go out. We are self-stimulating and self-designing creatures. Mencius, an ancient Chinese sage, concluded long ago that the mind works according to its own notion of the way it ought to work. In *The Mind in the Making* James Harvey Robinson put it this way: "The Greeks found that the mind could carry on an absorbing game with itself." Someone else has also said something of the same sort very neatly: Man is both the sculptor and the stone. And in the course of self-molding some individuals become fixed and rigid, while others manage to keep the possibilities of self-realization highly variable. This is one of the most important dimensions along which people differ, the dimension of rigidity-flexibility.

It appears to work like this. We may suppose that the bodily state represented at Stage 3 in Figure 1 is determined in part by the incoming sensory impulses and in part by the state of the nervous system existing at the time of arrival of the new sensory impulses. We may assume then that in the very rigid person, the state of affairs at Stage 3 is influenced far more by the conditions already existing than by any new sensory nerve currents being received. That is, stimulation from the outside has comparatively little effect. By comparison, we may suppose that the internal states of the flexible or adaptable individual are affected much more by new stimulation arising from environmental changes or happenings.

When we have moved along to a consideration of Stage 4, where most of the very important problems are to be more readily examined, we shall see a bit more clearly perhaps what is responsible for an individual's responsiveness, or rigidity. In the meantime it will be worth our while simply to sharpen our appreciation of the fact that people differ remarkably in the extent to which they are affected by the world about them—the environmental events at Stage 1— through the sensory stimulation at Stage 2. It is in this connection that we may understand in a peculiarly important sense the difference between a person who is "conservative," formal, governed by well-set habits, and a person who is experimental, spontaneous, adventurous. It would appear to involve, among other things, a difference in the electrical and chemical reactions at the sensory nerve endings and in the cell structures throughout the nervous system. Not that the difference is necessarily inborn or hereditary, in a physical or gene-carried sense; on the contrary, it is probably to a major degree in most cases the result of training and experience. It is apparently quite modifiable, but it is by no means superficial and easy to alter as a rule. A change in it constitutes a profound change in the person.

Aside from rigidity of this sort, there are certain frank disorders that can affect these pre-verbal stages of the communication process. Some of these disturbances are due to physical conditions. There can be faulty transmission of nerve currents, for example, with consequent failure of response, or inco-ordination of response, to stimuli. The reason for this may be due in some instances to damage to the nerve tracts resulting from injuries, infections or tumors, or to inherited defects. Difficulties of response seen in cases of poliomyelitis, or cerebral palsy, or in patients who have suffered cerebral hemorrhage, or stroke, are evidence of such nerve damage.

Blindness and deafness, partial or complete, are among the disorders that affect the functions of sensory impression found at Stages 2 and 3. In cases of impaired hearing, the cause may be located in the auditory division of the eighth cranial nerve, in the cochlea, or the inner ear, or in the external and middle portions of the ear. Infections can impair the workings of the eardrum and the tiny chain of bones that transmits the vibrations of the eardrum to the fluid that lies behind the thin membrane separating the middle part of the ear from the inner part. The nerve endings are bathed in this fluid, and it is generally assumed that when it vibrates they are correspondingly stimulated. In cases of total or nearly complete deafness, and in many cases of less severe impairment, the inner ear or the auditory nerve itself is assumed to be affected.

Under such circumstances, of course, outside events in the world of sound are not responded to for the good reason that they do not serve to a normal degree to set up nerve impulses. A wholly deaf person's knowledge of the world is a non-auditory, soundless knowledge. Likewise, a blind individual understands his surroundings without taking account of their visible qualities; he lives in a world known to him as sounds, odors, tastes, shades of warmth and cold, external pressures, and a welter of internal feelings. If we try to tell a deaf person about a symphony, or a blind man about a sky at dusk, we learn at least a little about the importance of the various sensory processes in providing a secure foundation of meaning, of *sense,* for our castles of words. When hearing and vision are in some degree impaired, the entire responding, evaluating, and communicating process is necessarily adjusted correspondingly.

The world we talk about to others and to ourselves is, so long as we talk sense, the world which we do, in fact, sense. And when we talk about this world we are understood by others in the ways in which their sensings have prepared them to understand what our own particular backgrounds of experience have prepared us to say. In testing the hearing of college students over many years, audiologists have found that about four or five out of every hundred have sufficient hearing loss to warrant examination by an ear specialist. One out of every hundred, on the approximate average, has a substantial loss of hearing. In older persons, of course, hearing comes to be much more commonly impaired. As most of us pass middle age and begin to enjoy the fruits of maturity, we can take for granted that for us the world of sound will be gradually muted, particularly in its higher registers. Impaired hearing, especially in its less severe forms, is to be appreciated as a Stage 2 disorder of widespread occurrence. So far from blandly taking for granted that he is being understood, the alert speaker takes due pains, first of all, to see to it that he is being heard. And the alert listener will check to determine whether he has heard correctly before deciding whether or not he agrees with what he assumes the speaker has said.

This all seems so offensively elementary that it is undoubtedly advisable to remind ourselves of the frequency with which these simple precautions are disregarded by our friends—and by us. Any teacher, preacher, or lawyer has been repeatedly astounded and dismayed by the demonstrated inefficiency of the spoken word as a means of communication. This is to be accounted for in part by the fact, which we have been considering, that a considerable proportion of the population—especially the adult and elderly segments of the population—suffers significant impairment of hearing. There are, however, at least two other reasons, undoubtedly more important than this one, why speech is as inefficient as it usually appears to be. One of these reasons is that many speakers take too much for granted: they assume they are being heard—and understood—when they are not, and so they do nothing to counteract the effects of the communicative failures and lapses, the blank moments and the misheard phrases, of which they are so innocently unaware.

The other of these reasons for the inefficiency of speech as a means of conveying information from one person to another is doubtless the most impressive and probably the most important of all. It is that listeners with perfectly good hearing—or impaired hearing for that matter—just don't always pay much attention to the speaker. Part of the time any representative member of the ordinary audience is simply not listening to the speaker at all. The most effective speakers, keenly aware of this, go to considerable pains to hold the listener's attention, and, even so, whenever they have anything of unusual importance to say they repeat it, in one way or another, over and over again. They never say, "But I have already told you!" when asked questions they have fully answered in the course of a lecture. They know so very well that while they may be reasonably sure they have *said* something, they can practically never be sure they have *told* it to anyone.

The lesson to be learned from this sort of experience is to

be gained as well, if not with even more striking effect, from writing a book and observing what its readers say about its contents. The words they sometimes put into the author's pencil are long to be pondered, and with widened eyes.

The old parlor game that is played by each person receiving a whispered message in his left ear and whispering it along, in turn, to the neighbor on his right, until the message has gone full circle, has amused millions and amazed the more thoughtful. What most of us appear not to have grasped quite as fully as we might have is the fact that something very much like this old parlor game, with its fantastic garbling of messages, is what goes on when the news of the world is gathered, sifted, condensed, and funneled through the channels of press, radio, and television day by day. Most of us, depending on fleeting pictures, short broadcasts, and briefer headlines, receive such a highly condensed account of the news each day that we are quite uninformed and misinformed much of the time. This is so easy to demonstrate, so often shown to be true, and so familiar to all of us in a personal sense that it can hardly be necessary to labor the point.

It is necessary, however, to labor the point's deep and pervasive significance. We are so completely accustomed to our eyes, ears, taste buds and other sensory equipment that we trust these frail and far from perfect instruments to an absurd degree. Moreover, we underestimate how important they are to us, nevertheless, in the acquisition and refinement of our knowledge. The Platonic and romantic traditions in our common philosophy have had the effect of persuading practically all of us, in varying degrees, to take for granted that we can and do gain much of our knowledge and wisdom by "intuition" or a "sixth sense" or in some other sort of mystical manner. The idea that our knowledge of the world must come through our sensory receptors, even the secondhand knowledge that we get through the spoken and printed words of other persons—and that these other persons, likewise, must derive their knowledge from their own sensings or, secondhand, from the verbal reports of the sensings of still other persons—this idea arouses a kind of self-defensive distrust in most of us whenever we are forced to face up to its hard reality and its implications. Consequently, it has been by no means commonly accepted in our culture. Most of us believe, with Plato, that what we can sense and know directly is a mere shadow of the Ideal, and that this alleged but taken-for-granted Ideal is somehow "much more real" than our sensings. This curious mysticism appears to affect us so strongly that most of us simply neglect our sensory equipment upon which, in fact, we do necessarily depend for our information about ourselves and our surroundings. Individually, we seem to know little about our sensory apparatus, and we appear to disregard very largely the role it plays in our basic orientation to our world and to life in general. Disregarding it to the extent we do results, of course, in some incredible beliefs and points of view, a great many of which even become crystalized in the shape of organizations and institutions.

It is to be realized, moreover, that with our imperfect knowledge and understanding of our sensory processes, we are readily subject to illusions and to individualistic distortions of perception. We sometimes experience a sheer failure of the sensory organs to function under conditions of neurosis or hysteria. One of the common symptoms of psychoneurosis, for example, is loss of hearing, or vision, or the sense of touch, although no physical impairment can be demonstrated. In other conditions of psychiatric significance sensory functioning is affected to the degree that genuine sensations are distorted or exaggerated in ways that make for illusions, or, in the absence of genuine relevant sensation, there are hallucinations—such as the well-known pink elephants on the familiar wall. In such ways the incoming stimulation is pathologically affected by conditions already existing at Stage 3 at the time of stimulation. And it would appear that such conditions already existing at Stage 3 are a function or result of factors operating at Stage 4, which we shall consider presently.

On the one hand, then, we trust our sense organs far more than is justifiable, and, on the other, we grossly underestimate their importance. The practical significance of these miscalculations is reflected in the regrettable consequences of our common tendency to be almost wholly unimpressed with the fact that we are quite entirely dependent upon our normally very limited, and our frequently defective, sensory processes for the functioning intelligence we are able to muster, "such as it is and what there is of it."

There are, then, two main types of disorder that occur at the second and third stages of the communication process as represented in Figure 1. The one is sensory impairment, or nerve damage, of a physical sort. The other, far more serious, is due to our failure to understand our sensory processes, whether normal or impaired. Relatively uninformed and with scant insight into these matters, we are subject to pathological self-deception as well as to the more common ravages of inattention and unbudging preconception. We suffer generally from a more or less habitual failure to check against the reality of sense the very much that we have been trained to take for granted.

Peering through the tiny, dusty windows of our senses, we see far less clearly than we imagine. Yet, dim as our vision may be, our destiny depends heavily upon it and what we make of it. We make of it what we do largely, it would seem, because of the meanings that lurk in the verbal forms and the specific symbols we are now about to examine and ponder. In the next several pages, then, we shall be preoccupied with whatever there may be about us that is human in any sense that matters very much.

... in these worlds of words inside our heads we hold ourselves captive.

CHAPTER ELEVEN

The Twig That Bends Itself

✳ The question of why we do the things we do divides contemplative men into several different schools. The champions of universal plan and purpose dispute with those who insist that in his dizzy ride on this whirling, dusty ball man is strictly on his own. The advocates of instinct are disbelieved by those who are impressed by the plasticity of the human fledgling and even of the balding adult. Those who doubt that only blood will tell base their skepticism on a conviction that as individuals we can learn vastly from experience. There are those who are convinced, indeed, that the twig can bend itself.

Yet, those with such a view as this are themselves divided into varied groups. There are many "laws" of learning. For our purposes, however, it is necessary to evaluate them only

95

in one respect. In one way or another most of them assume that we learn to do the things we do because we are *motivated* somehow to do them. Thorndike, Pavlov, Freud, Hull, and others too have, each in his own way and with his own pattern of emphasis, concluded that the reason we do what we do is that it is satisfying, it pays, it gratifies our needs, it reduces our drives, it enables us to escape punishments or to gain rewards. There would seem no reason to reject this fundamental principle. Yet, it does not appear to be sufficient.

Granted that we come to do most habitually those things which we find most rewarding, or least painful, there are still some important questions to be answered. For example, do we learn from experience to prefer the specific rewards we do prefer, or do certain physical drives such as hunger and thirst determine our preferences? This question further divides those who would explain the reasons for our behavior. In whatever way we may finally choose to answer the question, we are likely to gain from a steady contemplation of it the growing conviction that most of us are attracted by a very small variety of rewards, and we strive for them in only a few ways, quite unvarying and not remarkably ingenious. In addition to anything else we might say, then, in accounting for our behavior, it is surely to be concluded that, to an impressive degree, we do the things we do because we don't know any better.

If this would seem to elevate unduly the importance of our ignorance in the shaping of our lives, we may not, on this account, disregard it. Indeed, our simple rule, examined closely, seems like a summing up of much that has been said by Freud, and by all the others who have been professionally fascinated by "the unconscious." We may not dispose of the whole matter by supposing that "the unconscious," which Freud described as being intensely dynamic, is merely the same as our ignorance. Meanwhile, it is time we acknowledged our traditional mistake of supposing that our ignorance is not dynamic at all. The folk theory that what we don't know doesn't hurt us—even that ignorance is bliss—hardly squares with the facts of experience. While men have become more and more impressed by the power of their ideas, they have strangely overlooked the crushing force of the absence of ideas and the lack of information. "The unconscious," generally conceived in this spirit, may usefully be thought of as consisting in large part of all that the individual does not know, has never learned, has forgotten, or—and most especially—has come to take for granted. If this is what we mean by ignorance, then ignorance is a highly significant ingredient of "the unconscious." And it is a part of it that is rather more understandable—and plausible—than some of its other alleged aspects.

Certainly the contemplation of our ignorance can be a swift highway to wisdom. There seems no doubt that at least we are fools whenever we overvalue what we already know. Filling our own ears with all we have learned to say, we are deaf to what we have yet to hear. The searching out of what we have not yet learned, the remembering of things once known but since forgotten, the reviewing of all that is no longer seen for having been looked at so long, the re-questioning of long-accepted answers—these are means of escape from self-captivity. They are the techniques of awareness, the ways in which we can break out of "the unconscious." They are ways, therefore, of revising and increasing our possibilities of behaving, since only as we become aware of drives and assumptions hitherto unsuspected may we control and vary the motivations of our actions.

In the process diagramed in Figure 1 it is at Stage 4 that

"the unconscious" is most clearly to be regarded. This is to be understood particularly in the simple fact that most of us are quite unknowing of what goes on at Stage 4. The fundamental process that occurs there is a transformation—the transformation of the physiological goings-on at Stage 3 into symbols: words, sentences, numbers, diagrams, chemical formulae, mental pictures, tunes in the head, et cetera. We have previously wondered at this astonishing transformation, and it seems necessary to assume that the nature of it, the mode and mechanism of its occurrence, may not be divined soon, if ever. We are not obligated, however, to become benumbed. It is sensible under the circumstances to accept symbolization as a fact, as one of our bodily processes, and to observe and understand it to the best of our ability. The philosopher of science, Professor Gustav Bergmann, has said that although it is not necessary for us to understand digestion in order to digest our food, yet if more of us understood it better, there would be much less indigestion. In like vein it may be said that we are quite capable of symbolizing our experiences without knowing much about the process of symbolization, but there seems little doubt that if we understood the process much better than most of us do we would talk and listen and write and read ourselves into far less trouble than we do now.

There is no intention here to minimize our common knowledge about symbolization. After all, our education begins, and continues in large part, with the learning of reading, writing and the use of numbers. Speaking is a mode of symbolization taken all too much for granted, it is true, but in some schools at least the attempt is made to teach students to speak effectively. Music is not wholly neglected and there is some instruction provided in the graphic and plastic arts. In the colleges and professional schools the cultivation of the symbolic functions is carried, in some respects, to considerable lengths.

Even so, there is much we do not learn in school, save in courses seldom taught. In one special respect nearly all of us remain almost completely untutored: the use of a language, or any symbol system of whatever sort, necessarily involves an abstracting process, and this is something most of us either do not know at all or if we do we fail nonetheless to grasp very effectively its practical implications. This—this specific quantity of ignorance—would appear to be an aspect of our "unconscious" that is tremendously dynamic, giving rise very nearly continuously to effects of serious importance.

It is neither possible nor essential to give a complete account of symbolization and of abstracting at this point, but there are a few considerations that we need to emphasize duly. First of all, the physiological goings-on represented at Stage 3 in Figure 1 are "changed into" or "become" or "stimulate the occurrence of" the symbols—words or whatnot—that are to be found at Stage 4. This means that the symbols are different from the bodily processes, or feelings, or sensations, or the "facts," the events represented at Stages 1, 2 and 3. *What we say is not what we say it about.* This, as nearly everyone would suppose, is "obvious." Taking it to be "obvious," however, we tend to pay it no further mind.

In the meantime, we commonly act as though it were not obvious at all. Art galleries sometimes employ guards during certain exhibits in an effort to keep irate visitors from sticking walking canes and knives through the modernistic paintings which they evidently take to be something more than symbols. Perfume manufacturers, or their public-relations counselors, spend thousands of dollars picking the names which apparently millions of people react to as though they were buying names instead of odors. The numbers of parent-hours, to say nothing of grandparent-hours, spent annually in this or any other country deciding on names for babies are impressive evidence of the degree to which we take the name to be identical with what it names—as though the pockmarks of Homer would be the dimples of Danny Boy.

> *And canny is the nose that knows*
> *An onion that is called a rose.*

In this morning's paper is the pathetic story of a soldier's wife who was taken to a hospital in a state of profound shock, brought on *by being told* by a prankster that her husband had been killed in action.

". . . but words can never hurt me."

Our grandfathers killed and wounded one another in the duels they fought over the *words* no gentleman might allow to go unchallenged. What our grandfathers did as individuals we still do as nations—and occasionally as individuals too.

We talk about birds and bees when we mean men and women.

There are some subjects we don't discuss at all because we cannot find words we feel are proper.

Obvious as it may be that the word is not the thing, it is just as obvious that we very frequently react to the word as though it were the thing.

This we do because of a bit of dynamic ignorance—or a fundamental but largely unconscious assumption—operating at Stage 4: It may be that we do not always assume that the words we hear or read, or speak, or write are fully identical with what they are presumably about, but we often seem to take for granted that they are far more substantial than can be demonstrated.

By the canons of common sense this is not completely undesirable, of course. Part of the reason we survive as long as we do is that we tend to respond to "Fire!" as though it were blazing flame. In a world that is still made up of nations, we may be thankful that practically all the men, women and children in the United States respond to Old Glory as though it were much more than just a piece of bunting, and to "The Star-Spangled Banner" as if they took it to be something far more substantial than a mere pattern of sound waves created by clarinets and drums. It is fortunate that we can be trained to take poison labels seriously, to stop when confronted by red traffic lights, and to duck when a friend yells, "Duck!"

But like so many other blessings this one, too, is mixed. The rooster trained to respond to "Chickie, chickie, chickie!" as though it were really corn discovers one day that it also is the same thing as getting his head chopped off. Such clear cameos of tragedy should be far better lessons to us than they prove as a rule to be. The trained inclination to take the word "Danger" to be the thing it stands for keeps us out of zones of real danger; it is the same sort of trained inclination, however, that keeps us from enjoying the rewarding friendship of persons whose *names* we have been taught to hate or fear. The evaluting mechanism that enables us to love devotedly is the same one that makes us capable of wounding innocent strangers with our prejudices. It is the mechanism of identification, the trained habit of identifying words with things, of taking for granted that when we know a person's name, for example, or the name of his church, or country, or skin color, we know the person.

And so we do not respond to the person at all, because we respond to the name instead, as though it were the person. In doing this, of course, we tend to make the same response every time the name appears, and so we react to all Jews, all Negroes, all Mohammedans, all whites, and midgets, respectively, as though in each case they were all cut from the same dough with the same cooky cutter. This is the key to injustice—to cemeteries where only "Caucasians" may be buried, to auditoriums in which no Negro voices may ring out, to hospitals in which no doctors named Goldstein may work to save our lives, and, with equal tragedy, if with ironic justice, it is the key as well to Indias in which the Smiths and Alexanders may no longer conduct business quite as usual, and the South Africas in which folks with light complexions face an increasingly foreboding future.

This mechanism of identification, this general assumption that A is A, that "pigs is pigs" and business is business, this operates at Stage 4 and plays a very important part in determining the particular verbal responses, the statements or comments, we make at Stage 5. It is simply a basic or general characteristic of our language that it consists to a large degree of words that do not refer to anything specifically, but that are names for large categories or kinds of things and not for particular things.

This is a way of saying that there is a basic scheme of classification *built into* our common speech and language. This built-in classification system directs us so that we observe the things we can readily classify with the names we know, while we tend strongly to overlook or disregard everything else. We see with our categories. (In *Doubt and Certainty in Science,* J. Z. Young presents most intriguingly a theory much like this to the effect that the brain operates as a sort of selector and computer which classifies or sorts sensory inputs against a system of models and rules.) Because this is the case the specific experiences or feelings, the unique physiological events, at Stage 3 of Figure 1 are transformed at Stage 4 into symbols and patterns of symbols that do not mean very much in particular because they mean so much in general. We classify. We abstract. And so we talk about categories instead of individual persons or things or events. We make general statements about specific facts.

To the extent that we become conscious of this we become able to take it into account in evaluating what we say and in judging what is said to us. We become able more or less to control its effects, which are otherwise as likely to be bad as good. Becoming sensitive to how large or small a category is, to degrees of generality, to levels of abstraction, we develop antennae for detail, a sense of specificity, a nose for differences that make a difference, a knack of seeing far more clearly what we look at, and of saying much more exactly what we mean—unless we don't want to, and often, of course, there is no point in being precise. Precision can be boring and sometimes even stupid. Much of the charm of Omar Khayyám, the beauty of Keats, the depth of Shakespeare abide in their artful ambiguities. It is the ambiguities that are artless, or malicious—and that are, as such, so seldom charming or beautiful or profound—to which the wise man and the just are keenly sensitive.

So far we have hardly more than peeked furtively into the vast and lively inner world that exists like a fabulous unsuspected continent at Stage 4. There is more, amazingly more, to be come upon in this all but hidden realm within us, and as we proceed we must take pains not to lose ourselves in its darkening forests as we examine at least a few of their uncountable and not wholly knowable trees.

*Filling our own ears with all we have
learned to say, we are deaf to what we
have yet to hear.*

CHAPTER TWELVE

The Coins of Meaning

✳ The mysteries over which we are now maneuvering lie deep within ourselves, and yet we may be encouraged by the glimpses so far gained to believe that we might, with time and patience, discover enough about them to bring a kind of practical understanding within our stubby reach.

The fundamental trouble appears to be suggested by the fact that we use over and over again a quite small number of words to symbolize innumerable experiences or "facts," forever new, unique, never twice completely the same. Of course, there are ever so many differences that make no difference, and it can strain our tender qualities mightily to keep smiling in the company of compulsive hairsplitters who insist on telling us the time to the nearest second. But there are differences, like those between one blind child and another, for example, that no fair and intelligent person would knowingly overlook; there are times when what we had thought to be hairsplittings turn out to be the very discriminations upon which the Goddess of Justice herself depends; and in certain situations it would be a breach of scientific decorum and a mortal danger to all concerned to measure time only to the nearest second. And so, because it is sometimes essential, it is for all of us clearly desirable to understand how sufficient accuracy and due prudence are to be reasonably insured.

The answer has a good deal to do with vocabulary, not quite as we ordinarily think of it perhaps, but definitely vocabulary nonetheless. It is not that we need a very large vocabulary for most purposes, though it seems undeniable that there would be advantages in this, provided it were not too large. To demonstrate that one might be able to get along with the six hundred words of Basic English, or even with fewer words than that—as does a child who is just learning to talk—is not to prove that a larger vocabulary would not be better. Yet there is a limit beyond which a vocabulary becomes too big to be practical. It contains at last too many words that most people don't understand. Besides, it covers more subjects than anyone would have occasion to talk about without frittering away in needless prattle too many of the all too few precious hours of a single lifetime.

So far as most of us are concerned there are thousands upon thousands of words that are, with rare exceptions, better left in the dictionary where they won't be misused, waste time, and cause trouble.

With this granted, it is to be granted as well that most of

us would profit from adding very considerably to the supply of words we actually use and well understand. We need at least to be on the alert for new words—or new ways of employing old ones—that are being added continually to the common language we all unavoidably use.

Doubtless it would help us a bit, first of all, to add at least slightly to our personal vocabularies for talking about vocabulary itself. The word "word," for example, to choose a particularly important term, is impressively ambiguous— a working definition of it which some of my students and I once prepared for research purposes filled eight typewritten pages (it may be found in *Psychological Monographs,* Vol. 56, No. 2, 1944, pages 83-86). In an ingenious attempt to deal with the problems this ambiguity creates, Charles S. Peirce, one of the most important forerunners of the present-day scientific philosophers, clothed the terms "type" and "token" with relevant new meanings. He said in effect: Let us suppose that in writing a 100-word paragraph you use 60 different words; in this case, we shall say that you use 60 types in producing 100 tokens.

These words, "type" and "token," turn out to be very useful indeed to anyone who tries to understand the problems of vocabulary. I have used them, for example, in working out a measure of vocabulary that seems to get at something rather more dynamic than a mere estimate of the total number of words (types) a person "knows." I have called this new measure the type-token ratio, or TTR. (It is described in considerable detail in *Psychological Monographs,* Vol. 56, No. 2, 1944, and in the appendix of my *People In Quandaries,* New York: Harper & Brothers, 1946.) In the 100-word paragraph referred to above, in which we are to suppose that 60 different words were used, the ratio of types (different words) to tokens (total words) is 60:100, or .60.

The TTR may be computed for language samples of varied sizes, such as samples of 100 words, or 1,000, or 3,000 words, etc. The larger the sample, other things equal, the lower the TTR. This is true because we tend to "use up" our words—our types, that is—rather quickly when we talk or write continuously, so that while a person may use as many as 60 to 75 types in producing the first 100 tokens of a sustained discourse, he certainly is not able to keep this up indefinitely. An Iowa schoolgirl who wrote 18,000 words for us—in response to the general instruction to write about "whatever you want to write about"—was still adding a few new types in the eighteenth segment of 1,000 tokens, as shown in Figure 2. (John Chotlos, *Psychological Monographs,* Vol. 56, No. 2, 1944.) She used 434 different words (types) in writing the first 1,000 words (tokens), introduced 298 new types in the second 1,000 tokens, 204 in the third 1,000, 239 in the fourth, 201 in the fifth, 172 in the tenth, 83 in the fifteenth, and 59 in the eighteenth 1,000 tokens. Had she continued writing presumably she would have demonstrated that her vocabulary was, in principle, inexhaustible. Nevertheless, she exhibited the bulk of her working store of words rather quickly. By the time she had written the first 6,000 tokens, the first one-third of the sample, she had already introduced more than half of the 3,025 types she used in producing the entire 18,000-word passage.

In doing this she was probably representative of people generally. In saying this it is to be granted, of course, that we seldom—most of us never—speak or write continuously until we have produced as many as 18,000 words about any particular subject, or at any one sitting. For the most

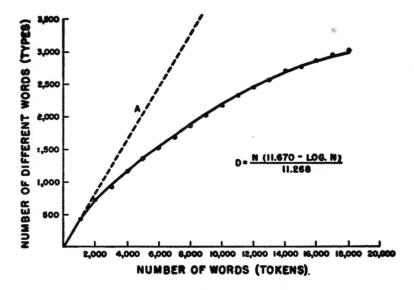

$$D = \frac{N \; (11.670 - LOG. \; N)}{11.268}$$

NUMBER OF DIFFERENT WORDS (TYPES)

NUMBER OF WORDS (TOKENS).

FIGURE 2. The dots along the solid line in this graph represent the numbers of different words, shown along the left-hand margin, used by an Iowa schoolgirl in writing 1,000 words, 2,000 words and so on, shown along the base line, for a total sample of 18,000 words. The writer used 732 different words in producing her first 2,000 words, 1,175 different words in writing her first 4,000 words, etc., up to 3,025 different words in producing the total sample of 18,000 words. The rate at which she introduced new words into the sample fell off as she went along, as shown by the dots along the solid curve, and as represented by the equation which describes this curve. The broken line A shows the rate at which the schoolgirl would have introduced new words into the sample had she continued to introduce them as fast as she did for the early part of the sample. The graph is discussed in the accompanying text. (Reprinted, as modified by adding the dotted line A, by permission of the author, John W. Chotlos, and publisher, the American Psychological Association, Inc., from *Psychological Monographs*, Vol. 56, No. 2, 1944, p. 106.)

part we fire verbal popguns. We seldom talk long enough at a time to reveal anything like the full extent of our vocabularies. Speaking briefly, a few words at a time, we tend to use a relatively few types over and over again. No matter how many thousands of words we may "know," therefore, we get along day in and day out for the most part with only a few hundred, at most a few thousand, types. Indeed, in one of our studies (Helen Fairbanks, *Psychological Monographs*, Vol. 56, No. 2, 1944) just 46 different words made up 50 per cent of the sample of 30,000 running words produced by ten university freshmen in giving orally their interpretations of common proverbs. A group of ten psychiatric patients, diagnosed as having schizophrenia, used only 33 types in producing half of their total sample of approximately 30,000 words in the same study. In another study (Mary Mann, *Psychological Monographs*, Vol. 56, No. 2, 1944), in which the persons examined wrote their life stories, a sample of 67,200 words was obtained from a group of 24 university freshmen and a like sample was secured from a group of 24 schizophrenic patients. The patients used only 95 different words (types) to produce 50 per cent of their total number of tokens, while the freshmen used 96 types to arrive at half of their total sample. For both groups ten types—*only ten different words*—made up 25 per cent of the total of 67,200 words! For the freshmen these ten words were *the, I, and, to, was, my, in, of, a, it.* With the exception of *we* instead of *it*, the same ten words headed the list for the patients also. The great bulk of our daily language is certainly made up of words of one syllable, and astonishingly few of them.

Considered mathematically, in study after study, this fact that so very few words carry such an enormous share of our total verbal load comes to seem almost too impressive to grasp. To think that in writing over 67,000 words about their own life histories, even a group of university students actually used only ten different words to make up one-fourth of that total—over 16,000 tokens—and less than 100 different words to produce half of the total—over 33,000 tokens—is to be driven close to the conclusion that we are very nearly senselessly repetitive and monotonous. We use so few different words in producing the greater part of our speech and writing that it seems hard to believe that we could possibly succeed in communicating anything to one another except the most commonly accepted views and information and universally shared feelings. One wonders whether, with so few words, and with their having been used millions upon millions of times, it is really possible, or ever will be again, to say anything completely new. One is tempted to suppose that, however absurd the idea may have seemed to us the first time we heard of it, enough monkeys with enough typewriters could indeed quite easily by sheer chance produce duplicates of all the books we have ever written.

There are yet other ways of pointing up this heavy duty that is done by the spindly underpinnings of the structure of our language. In her study, Dr. Fairbanks took a second look at the 100 most frequently occurring words in each of her samples of language. She found that these 100 words made up 68.32 per cent of the total number of words used by the schizophrenics, and that the 100 different words most frequently employed by the freshmen constituted 62.91 per cent of all their words. In a study of 500 telephone conversations involving roughly 80,000 words (H. R. French, C. W. Carter, Jr., and W. Koenig, Jr., "The Words and

Sounds of Telephone Conversation," *Bell System Technical Journal,* 1930, 9, 290-324) the 100 most frequently used words made up 75 per cent of the total sample! Without going further into detail, it is clear that very few words— types, that is—serve us for the greater part of our speaking and writing. Viewed in this manner, our vocabularies can only be described as meager.

Yet there is, we may be sure, something at least a trifle deceptive about all this. What are we to do with the fact that there are over 600,000 words in the English language? It is, indeed, a most significant fact. And the end is not yet. There are new words "happening every day." Our common language is an ever-widening pool, filled solely by our own verbal sweat, each bead distilled from experience that is ours uniquely. No day comes and goes on which no new beads fall into the pool. The "sea of words" around us is of our own creation—our own exudation, no less—and wide as it has come to be it will certainly never cease to become ever more vast.

In one of our investigations, the one by Dr. Chotlos, we caught some particularly intriguing glimpses of this seeming inexhaustibility of man's verbal fertility. Dr. Chotlos drew several curves showing the relationship between the number of tokens and the number of types in his language samples. These curves all rise essentially like the solid line shown in Figure 2, and although they bend, becoming flatter as they are extended, they do not, within the limits of our data—or of our imagination—wholly cease to rise. That is to say, if such a curve as the one in Figure 2 were projected indefinitely on and on, so far as we can know or imagine it would continue indefinitely to rise, less and less to be sure, but always to some degree, however slight. It seems necessary to suppose that even after a million billion tokens had been uttered, if then another thousand, or ten thousand, or perhaps another million words were to be spoken, at least a few new types would be added in the speaking of them. Such a curve and such ponderings leave us believing quite simply that language "lives and grows." It has about itself a sort of organic unity and independence. It lives, so to speak, in its own way. A language, therefore, may not be learned and employed innocently, without consequences. It does things on its own account. It does things to us who use it. It accentuates incredibly the effects of the slight physical effort we make in order to speak and so it is that as we make in our throats the sounds of language, we are blown by winds of our own blowing.

Beyond what we have so far said, however, are the arresting implications of the mathematical equation in Figure 2 and of the particular shape of the curve. Just the bald fact that the changing ratio of the number of different words (types) to the total number of words (tokens) in a person's language output can be precisely described—as precisely at least as Dr. Chotlos described it with the mathematical equation shown in Figure 2—is very sobering. It suggests, as does a very considerable mass of other data accumulated in recent years, that there may well be a machinelike quality to our language behavior. With respect, at least, to the question of how many different words a speaker will use in producing a thousand, or five thousand, or ten thousand running words, the outcome, once we know his word-production pattern, would seem to be nearly as predictable as it would be if we were dealing with a robot or a "mechanical brain."

True, this need not imply that meanings are equally predictable and that in making evaluative judgments we are necessarily as machinelike as we are in grinding out words. The set-screw precision we tend to exhibit in maintaining a particular rate of change in the ratio of types to tokens does, however, compel any thoughtful person to re-examine language in its major aspects. As individuals, we are inclined, for example, to think of our own language as being, in fact, our very own. We chuckle over *our* snappy comebacks, we remember long and repeat ever so often the clever, or profound, or apt remarks *we* have made. And in a sense they are ours, and each is, in its own circumstance and implication, unlike any other utterance ever made in all the world's voluble history. Yet, each is, at the same time, in its basic form, as a copy made from an ancient stencil, so far as concerns the sounds and words of which it is composed, and— far more than we should like to believe, no doubt—even the meanings to be extracted from it.

Professor S. I. Hayakawa, along with other semanticists, has made particularly effective use of the word "psittacism" in commenting upon our verbal behavior. The word is suggested by the Greek term for "parrot," from which we get the word "psittacosis" which means "parrot fever." A psittacism is a statement that is made in a parrotlike fashion, a parroting or repeating of something one has read or been told. We may speculate on the intriguing question of how much of our daily conversation is made up of psittacisms. At breakfast we read the paper, or on the way to work we listen to the news—and the commercials—that come to us from the car radio. Maybe instead we ride a bus to work and on the way our seat neighbor tells us what he knows and thinks and feels about taxes, prices, his landlord, his son's teachers, and the United Nations.

"Man said the cost of living is up two points. Don't understand how things can go on like this."

"Artie Shaw's back from England, I see."

"It's Michigan State over Notre Dame by two touchdowns."

"They got aluminum foil at Gimbels again."

"Duz does everything."

"Betty's back but Bob's staying in Kansas City for the week end."

"Saw Jim this noon and he said Williams doesn't stand a chance unless the vote is heavy."

"L.S.M.F.T."

"Iowa City's a swell place to live."

"I guess ole Turtle is really subversive all right."

How much of this gets repeated—by you, by me, by all of us—and how many times during how many days? Like a pebble tossed into a pond, so a remark tossed into our common pool of talk makes ripples. How large are they in a specific case, how far do they travel, and how long do they last? One day several years ago I composed a limerick and told it to some friends. Two weeks later it was told to me by a man who had heard it a few days before several hundred miles away in Mississippi. It would be interesting to know how many times the limerick has been repeated since, by how many persons, and how many times each one of them has repeated it—the first year, and the second, and the third, and so on—with what sort of curve of diminishing, or cumulative, frequency, and with what sorts of variations in this curve for various parts of the country, for different occupational groups, varying educational levels and social classes. To what extent, in other words, is our society infested, if that is a fair word, with psittacisms? With what specific psittacisms more than others?

As such questions flit by they can hardly leave us completely unaffected. Just to be introduced to the word "psittacism" is to be moved to wonder about the degree to which one's own speech is made up of parrotings. Any statement we make that is a literal repetition, or a close paraphrasing, of something we have heard or read is a psittacism. There must be individuals, or so it certainly seems, whose speech consists of nothing but psittacisms. With a sufficient awareness of the tremendous prevalence of psittacisms, we come at last to feel grateful when they are at least fresh. And when we have learned to appreciate fresh psittacisms, today's instead of yesterday's, we are impressed, in a new way that seems at first truly strange, by those extraordinary remarks that are not psittacisms at all, but that are original, things said for the very first time! The world *première* of a significant sentence—especially one of our own—becomes for us an occasion for the experiencing of new and delightful appreciations.

And so we find it possible to realize how machinelike our language behavior can, and very often does, become. Remarks that are not psittacisms are rare. Words that have never been spoken before are rarer still, rare enough for us to be thrilled by them if only we understand how rare they are. To invent a word is to perform an act of creation that sets one apart, beyond all quibble, from all those living things that cannot make a word.

Yet there is, as we said a few pages back, something at least a trifle deceptive about all this. The key to what there is that might be misleading about it is the fact that such a curve as the one shown in Figure 2 has a particular shape. It bends. And it bends in a certain way. If you will turn again to Figure 2 you will observe that the dotted line, *A*, has been drawn as an extension of the first small part of the curve. This dotted line shows what the type-token ratio—

the ratio of different words to total words—would have been had it continued to be the same throughout the language sample as it was during the first 1,000 words. You will remember that 434 different words were used by the schoolgirl who was doing the writing in producing these first 1,000 tokens. Had she kept this up she would have used slightly over 3,000 types in producing the first 7,000 tokens; as it actually turned out, however, she used only 1,700 types. The difference between 3,000 and 1,700 is the difference between the broken line *A* and the solid line in Figure 2. It indicates how much the solid curve bends.

The bend in this curve means that there are, in a general sense, two kinds of words in our language, those that are used about as much by one person as another and those that are used much more and in greater variety by some individuals than by others. In the first category there are the words—such as the ten one-syllable words that made up one-fourth of Dr. Mann's samples—that are employed necessarily by everyone who uses the language. Moreover, they are quite unavoidably used about equally often, comparatively, by all of us.

In Dr. Fairbanks' samples 100 different words accounted for roughly two-thirds of the total verbal output. This was true for both her groups, the college students and the schizophrenic patients. Dr. Mann also listed the 100 words that occurred most often in each of her language samples. It is very important in this connection that not only were the language samples studied by Dr. Fairbanks and Dr. Mann different in that they were produced by different individuals, but also in the one case the language was spoken and in the other it was written; moreover, Dr. Fairbanks had her subjects interpret proverbs and Dr. Mann instructed hers to write their life stories. Even so, when their various lists of 100 most frequently used words are compared, it turns out that 69 of the 100 words are common to both lists, written and spoken, for the college freshmen, and 64 of the 100 are common to both lists for the mental hospital patients. Moreover, of the 100 most frequently occurring words in the spoken samples of the freshmen and the schizophrenic patients, respectively, 79 appear in both lists, and 83 words are common to the 100 most frequently used words in the respective written samples of the two groups. It is to be suspected, on the basis of such findings, that within broad limits the bulk of our words is largely the same regardless of who is writing or talking or what is being discussed. The findings of Fairbanks and Mann, and of other investigators as well, seem to mean that probably not more than a third to a half of our speech or writing, and possibly quite a bit less than that, serves clearly to express our individualities, so far as the use of words is for each one of us distinctive.

With respect to vocabulary, then, it appears that one person is not much different from another so far as the 100 or so most commonly used words are concerned—and this means so far as probably about two-thirds of the total verbal output is concerned. These 100 or so very common words may be thought of as "language links," so to speak. That is, they are largely words like *and, in, of, to,* etc., that do not serve as distinctive names of things, or as vivid verbs, or modifiers, but fundamentally as fasteners that hold together the net of language itself. They have to be used, therefore, by anyone who speaks the language—and the use of anything that is employed by everyone distinguishes no one.

It is in the use of uncommon words—or of common words in uncommon ways—that individuality is expressed. Therefore, if we were to eliminate, first of all, the 100 words, more or less, that do not serve very well to differentiate anyone from anyone else, and were then to compute the type-token ratio—the ratio of total words to different words—for the remaining part of our speech, we would probably find great differences between one speaker and another. And these differences should be quite important for what they would indicate with regard to intelligence and personality in a peculiarly functional sense. A vocabulary adroitly employed and richly varied in its distinctive parts is certainly to be distinguished, for its effects and personal implications, from one that is meager beyond the common store of basic words and that is rigidly applied.

There are, we see, two quite different aspects of vocabulary. There is the common vocabulary that we all possess, the "little words" that are necessary but not distinctive. There is also, however, the great bulk of vocabulary, estimated by the late Professor Robert Seashore (*Psychological Bulletin,* 1933, 30, 709-710) as running close to 70,000 different words for the average college undergraduate. From this bulk we draw the types that make up perhaps a third of all our tokens, the individualistic third of all we say or write. This is the part of our vocabulary that is made up of the less common words. They, and the one-third or so of our speech for which they are responsible, account to a significant degree for the fact that no two of us speak or write in quite the same way. Each of us can be identified by his language quite as surely as by his fingerprints, if only his language is examined closely enough. And those who seek for the meaning of what used to be called "the soul" and what in these days we speak of, as though our understanding were deeper, as "the personality," may very well not do better than to search exhaustively for all that is associated with each person's verbal individuality.

The statement just made to the effect that about a third of our verbal output serves to express our individuality may be somewhat optimistic, and undoubtedly it is overly neat. The probability that it is optimistic was suggested several years ago by the findings of Professors Paul Witty and M. Fry, who studied the language used by college students in writing themes. (*Journal of Educational Psychology,* 1929, 19, 135-138.) When the language the students used was compared with the Thorndike word-count (*The Teacher's Word Book,* by E. L. Thorndike, New York: Teachers College, Columbia University, 1921) it was found that roughly 85 per cent of their words were among the 1,000 most commonly used words, according to the Thorndike list. The practical meaning of this is indicated more or less by some of the basic information provided by Professor Ernest Horn's analysis of five million running words taken from common written materials. (Horn, E., *A Basic Writing Vocabulary: 10,000 Words Most Commonly Used in Writing.* Iowa City: University of Iowa Monographs in Education, No. 4, 1926.) Professor Horn found that just three words, *the, and,* and *to,* made up 10 per cent of the sample of five million running words he studied! Ten different words made up 25 per cent of the total, as was the case in the Mann study, previously cited. Fifty types comprised 47 per cent, 100 types about 60 per cent, 500 different words 85 per cent, and the 1,000 most common words made up 90.4 per cent of the total. The most common 4,000 words accounted for 97.8 per cent and the most common 4,500 for 98.1 per cent of the five million running words. All of which means that if 85 per cent of the students' words in the Witty and Fry study were drawn from the 1,000 most common Thorndike words (the Thorndike and Horn lists are more or less similar so far as present purposes are concerned) there could hardly have been a very great deal about their respective verbal usages that was sharply individualistic.

Such facts suggest rather forcefully that probably even less than one-third of our verbal output distinguishes us in any very significant way as individual users of language.

An interesting side light on all this is to be seen in the fact that ever since the late Professor Thorndike compiled his famous count of the most commonly used words, the editors and publishers of elementary schoolbooks have been manufacturing a product strangely new under the literary sun. They have been "constructing" school readers in which children in the early grades are introduced first to the words most frequently used, followed in orderly progression by words of decreasingly frequent usage. Now, among our most common words, of course, are *in, to, of, and, as,* and the like, together with most of the pronouns, a few nouns, adjectives and adverbs, and a small supply of verbs. (Incidentally, we found in one of our studies that one-fourth of all the verbs in a total of several thousand written words were forms of only one verb, *to be—is, am, are, was,* etc.)

The trouble is not—as it was with the stutterer who had learned to say "Peter picked a peck of pickled peppers"— that these most common words are hard to work into a conversation. The trouble is that a sensible conversation, to say nothing of a thrilling or significant one, is hard to "make out of" these words. It is extraordinarily difficult to arrange them in ways that result in stories that are "either true or delightful." They are in general the words that do not serve to differentiate one sample of language from another.

Nor may we safely assume that the more frequently a word is used by people generally the more "simple" it is for a child to grasp. The fact is, of course, that for every first-grader who can give a clearly satisfactory definition of *and* or *to* or *of*—words that can be defined well only by expert semanticists—there are doubtless thousands who can do quite well in giving an account of what they might mean by *elephant* or *newspaper* or *refrigerator*. The "little words" may—or may not—be especially easy for a child to "see," to recognize as visually perceived designs, but it is by no means certain that they are especially easy to comprehend. They are essential, certainly, and children must use them, whether they "understand" them or not, if they are to speak, write, read, or listen to the mother tongue. If they are to speak or write it well, however, and if they are to evaluate it duly, they must learn more than the "little words." Indeed, if they are to use even the "little words" with significance they must learn to employ, with discrimination and with a comprehensive sense of language structure, a host of other words to go with them.

What is to be appreciated above all else, of course, is that children have need of a *liking* for reading and writing, a *feeling* for the words they themselves speak, a *sensitivity* to the sound or melody and especially to the sense of the words they hear. Whether this feeling, this sensitivity for language, can ever be cultivated—indeed, whether it manages not to be emaciated—by a systematic preoccupation with the "little words" is something of which we need to be abundantly assured, for it seems to be by no means clearly plausible. Just as writing is obviously more than a matter of finger flexing or motor co-ordination, so reading is much more than the activation of eye muscles or mere visual perception.

Writing and reading are modes of symbolic functioning, and for the doing of them the brain—and the endocrine glands—are enormously more important than either the hand or eye. Reading is something we do, not so much with our eyes, as such, as with our knowledge and interests and enthusiasms, our hatreds and fondnesses and fears, our evaluations in all their forms and aspects. Because this is so, a fondness for reading is something that a child acquires in much the same way as he catches a cold—by being effectively exposed to someone who already has it. He is most likely to catch it from a parent or teacher or favorite uncle who loves to read, or else quite by himself from an author who loves to write, and who lets the prepositions fall where they may.

In pursuing a curiosity about vocabulary we come in ways such as these upon many and many a clue to humanness. Words are, of course, among the very ancient and certainly the most significant of mankind's inventions, and still our knowledge of them is far from plentiful. More is known, nevertheless, very much more, than has been summarized or intimated in these pages.

For the present, it is mainly to be considered, as we have been at pains to understand, that our common vocabulary is a great community storehouse of words, from which there is given to each child who learns the language a basic set of types. These he will use all his life over and over again as the tokens of his meanings. He may select from the storehouse a few, or very nearly none, or ever so many additional types, or words, over and above those in the basic set. And it is in the choices he makes of these extra words, as well as in the particular uses he makes of all his words, that he exhibits—and refines—his distinctive character as a human individual.

Before we break off our ruminations about words and vocabularies, there is a glance to be cast at the all too meagerly considered Dark Age of speech development that extends from the birth cry to "the first word." The very nearly unbroken succession of events with which it is filled is of an order of importance which probably few of us suspect, and which even those who are learned in such matters have only recently come to appreciate with due wonder.

A child learns to play by ear the strange sound-making throat chords with which he comes equipped into this noise-filled world—which he in turn helps to fill, by the measure of his own small mite, more full with noise than he finds it to be on his arrival. Professor Orvis C. Irwin of the Iowa Child Welfare Research Station has listened with a scientific ear to more babies making more vocal sounds than had been observed by all other like-minded investigators put together in the hundred years or so since 1851, when one Dr. Lobische published what was probably the first public report of such observations of the speech sounds of infants. From the mass of data he has accumulated, Professor Irwin has concluded that babies begin very early, no later indeed than the birth cry, to learn the rudiments of speech.

During the first ten days of life over nine out of ten sounds produced by infants approximate the sound of *a* as in *hat* or *cat*. From this monotonous but promising beginning, the average infant who is destined to wind up speaking English, or American English, proceeds to acquire mastery in due time over the twelve vowels, five diphthongs, and twenty-five consonants of the English tongue. (These generally accepted numbers can be enlarged considerably or even reduced, of course, for particular purposes and the three categories of sounds, or phonemes, given here can be broken down into a number of sub classes.) By the age of six months the average baby has "discovered" most of the vowels and about half the consonants. By the age of twelve months, at least half the babies beside whose play pens Professor Irwin kept his vigil were producing eighteen different sounds; by two years they had increased this to twenty-five; and when Professor Irwin folded his notebook and silently stole away just as the toddlers were rounding two years and a half, they—half of them, that is—were making twenty-seven different sounds. The most advanced ten per cent were producing thirty-one. The average six-year-old has yet to bring under control the last three or four phonemes that he will eventually call his own.

Boys do not quite keep pace with girls in the rate at which they master the different speech sounds, and the girls—even in infancy—tend to make more use of the sounds they are able to make. They spend more time making them. Mental retardation, in children studied by Professor Irwin in an institution for "the feeble-minded," is associated with a clear retardation in the rate of mastery of the sounds of speech. (This does not mean, incidentally, that a child who is slow in developing speech is necessarily mentally retarded; there are many reasons why a child may acquire speech at a subdued rate.) Children who are deaf are also delayed in developing the phonemic elements. There is a tendency, too, for normal youngsters whose parents are on the lower educational and economic levels to progress more slowly in learning speech sounds than children from the higher levels. Professor Irwin has attempted in some cases to speed up the progress of children in families on the lower socioeconomic strata by the simple method of having their parents read stories to them, and he has found that they do, indeed, respond to this increased language stimulation, even when scarcely more than one year old. They respond by doing more sound making, indulging in more vocal play, and by increasing the rate at which they learn the individual phonemes.

In general, Professor Irwin and his fellow investigators have done the parents of the world the tremendous service of indicating that the vocal playfulness, babbling, cooing and general making of speech sounds during the first year of infancy are far more important in the child's eventual speech development than had been realized. Not that defenseless babies are justifiably to be prodded, bribed, and provoked into cooing and babbling from morning till night every day of their innocent lives. More children are made nervous, tense, shy, and otherwise emotionally disabled by parents who are fussy, grim, and unrelenting in "bringing them up" than by parents who are less vigilant and even in many cases somewhat negligent. The ideal parent is aware of the normal rates of the many aspects of child development, understands the tremendous differences among children—or shown by any particular child from circumstance to circumstance—within the wide limits of these normal rates, and is sufficiently skilled and affectionate in providing encouragement so as not to indulge in threatening and demoralizing nagging.

So far as this problem of the promotion of normal speech development is concerned, there would be much to be said for an organization, with motivations somewhat like those of the Gideon Bible Society, that would place a copy of Professor Charles Van Riper's delightful little book, *Teach-*

ing Your Child to Talk (Harper & Brothers, 1950), beside every bed in every maternity ward in the country for every new mother—and father—to read. Professor Van Riper is a distinguished and trusted speech pathologist who writes with a feeling for his subject that marks him as a literary craftsman, as well as an authority who understands deeply what he is writing about, and what he is writing about is much more important than can be made quite clear—even to those of us who take for granted that we know what we mean when we recite the psittacism that to be human is to speak.

Teaching our children to talk is by no means a simple undertaking. Our extravagant bungling of it is indicated by the fact that children with speech disorders make up one of our very largest handicapped groups—at least three million of school age in our own country, counting only those who are most seriously affected—many more than the blind and deaf and those with cerebral palsy and polio all put together. Moreover, as one of our own studies has shown, only one out of ten university freshmen claims to be free of stage fright, and he is counterbalanced by one who is gravely incapacitated by speech fear. The other eight are in between, contending with degrees of uneasiness between slight and panicky.

Although as infants most children coo and babble with a delight that is all-engaging, by the time they have run the gamut of the elementary and high-school grades, the act of speaking audibly in the presence of their fellows has been transformed, by some cultural or pedagogical witches' brew, into a baffling and unnerving ordeal. Surely nothing else in the whole unlovely catalog of our child rearing mayhems and missed opportunities is more tragic in its retarding effect on man's struggle to rise above the level of the dumb brute. We appear to cherish more feebly than seems possible the wondrous realm of human promise to which the child's sounding glottis is the enchimed doorway.

But there is time, no end of time so far as we may know. A day will surely come when those who bring the children in the world, and those who make its strange ways known to them, will understand the art of teaching them how to play wonderfully well and with enchantment the exquisite instruments of speech by which they are endowed. We can only believe that day will be better—better by far than the time of our lives, better even than the golden time that never was which men have always cherished as the good old days.

. . . as we make in our throats the
sounds of language, we are blown by winds
of our own blowing.

CHAPTER THIRTEEN

Are There Really Gilligs?

✳ The forty-two sounds of standard American speech which we learn early in life are the basic units by means of which we come to transform our experiences into words. For purposes of writing and reading, their counterparts are the twenty-six letters of the English alphabet. With these basic units we form the 600,000 words, more or less, of the English language. Actually, as we have considered, no individual makes use, even rarely, of more than a small proportion of all these words, and we probably do two-thirds or more of our speaking and writing with scarcely more than a mere hundred of them. Nevertheless, the total number of different words man has invented is very imposing and it grows more impressive day by day.

These phonemes and letters and words are the threads of sound and line from which the fabric of language is loomed. And in the weaving of it there are patterns, a circumstance that brings to mind Amy Lowell's undying question: "Christ, what are patterns for?" Though we are no more likely to answer this question fully than we are to forget it wholly, we are moved by contemplation of it to be more sensitive than we might otherwise be to the effects that patterns have—and to the possibilities, if only we let ourselves explore them, of making patterns, new and unlike those we know, with effects more to our liking.

The patterns of language are what we examine and try to understand in the realms of logic and grammar, or syntax, although during our school days we may not have appreciated deeply the truth of this and its profound significance. We shall forgo the luxury of a full-scale exploration, or re-exploration, of the neat complexities of syllogistic reasoning and of the canons and fashions of grammar, but there are a few modest excursions that we shall doubtless enjoy making into these primly plotted regions.

Logic consists of rules for drawing inescapable conclusions from given premises. There are three very basic rules:

The first is that a gillig is a gillig.

The second is that anything is either a gillig or it is not a gillig.

The third is that anything cannot be both a gillig and not a gillig.

So, of anything you please you will say, if you are logical, that either it is a gillig or it is not, and that if it is a gillig then it is a gillig, because it can't be a gillig and also not be a gillig.

All this is true as it can be—because we say it is. So long

as we all agree to this, that is all there is to it. That is how it is with rules. Like the rules of football or canasta. How do you know it counts six points for your team if you carry the football across the goal line? How can you prove this? It says as much in the rule book. How can you be sure that a red three counts 100? Somebody wrote it in a book of canasta rules, and we agree not to make a fuss about it. So we all pretend that a red three counts 100, and that a touchdown (a United States touchdown, that is, and until further notice) counts six points, just as we all pretend that 2 plus 2 equals 4, there are nine players on a baseball team, and the term of office of the President of the United States is four years—and, if we like, that a gillig is a gillig. All these are certainly true, for the curiously good reason that we agree they are. They are not usually true, or generally, or largely, or probably true. They are true, period. Because we say so.

They are examples of truth by convention. That is, it is as though all the people concerned were to go to a big convention, and someone were to say, "I move that we all agree that 2 plus 2 equals 4." If someone else were to say, "I second the motion," and the chairman, after due ritual, were to call out, "All in favor signify by saying, 'Aye!' " and everybody were to shout, "Aye!" then "2 plus 2 equals 4" would be true. In fact, if before this came up it had been agreed that a majority vote was to be taken as deciding any question, then even if only 51 per cent of those voting had shouted, "Aye!" "2 plus 2 equals 4" would have become a truth—by convention.

Our society, any society, is bound together—in some respects, tied down—by such truths by convention. Another name for them is *formal* truths, as distinguished from *factual* truths. Still other names for them are laws, or rules and regulations. And what the wise men of our culture understand very clearly is that the rules by which we live, or try to, are cast crudely or well in the basic molds of the three great laws of logic we stated a few lines ago:

1. A gillig is a gillig, or pigs are pigs, or 2 equals 2—or, in general terms, A is A. This is the law of identity.

2. Anything must be either a gillig or not a gillig, pigs or not pigs, 2 or not 2—or, in general terms, A or not-A. This is the law of the excluded middle.

3. Something cannot be both a gillig and not a gillig, pigs and not pigs, 2 and not 2—or, in general terms, A and not-A. This is the law of non-contradiction.

These three basic rules of our symbolic lives are seldom expressed this way in so many words, but they are silently taken for granted, more or less consciously or unconsciously, by practically everyone under nearly all circumstances. They have been distilled from the long ages of man's experience. We may hardly quarrel with them. To say flatly and without qualification that they are not true would be to make a statement as interesting to a psychiatrist as to a logician. It is to be understood, of course, that they represent only a certain kind of truth. They represent truth by convention, by social agreement, the kind of truth that is taken as truth by common consent of those concerned.

This, of course, is a kind of truth altogether different from factual truth, from dependable statements about the so-called realities of direct experience. It is true that 2 equals 2, but not that 2 bananas equal any other 2 bananas. The statement that 2 equals 2—put just like that, without qualification, just 2 in general and another 2 in general—is not a statement about the world of fact and living experience at all. A true statement about the world might be that 2 bananas equal 6 bananas.

It is very likely that a great deal, perhaps even most, of the serious trouble within us and among us comes about because we fail to notice the difference between formal truth and factual truth—and so we take 2 equals 2 to mean the same as 2 doctors equal 2 doctors, or 2 Americans equal 2 Americans, or 2 dollars equal 2 dollars.

The point not to be missed—and we all but make a practice of missing it—is that "2 equals 2" is a formal truth and a factual falsehood. It can also serve as a practical convenience, provided the degree to which it is a factual falsehood is appreciated and allowed for whenever we try to apply it in actual instances.

Now, 2 equals 2, or A equals A, is the formula by means of which we act as though the world were made up of categories, or types, or groups, or classes of things. Something has to be either a gillig or not a gillig—we say. And if it is a gillig, well then, it is a gillig. The nonsense word, gillig, is used in these sentences only to make them seem less nonsensical than they might otherwise appear to be. For example, if we were to say that everyone has to be either a genius or not a genius, we might immediately begin to have doubts and raise questions, because we know from experience that people vary a great deal, so that not only are any two so-called geniuses not alike by any means but, moreover, one and the same person can appear to be a genius, an idiot, and a rather average sort of fellow all within the space of a few moments. On top of that, we realize that the man I call a genius is a man you may call a dolt. And we are likely to have all this come to mind when we are told that everyone has to be either a genius or not, and that if you are a genius, well then, you are a genius. This, we say, may be logical, but it doesn't seem very useful or make wholly satisfactory sense. But a gillig? That's different. It may very well be not only true but also highly important that a gillig is a gillig. Who knows?

In order to be logical we must first agree that there are certain categories, or classes, or pigeonholes into which all people, or things, or experiences are to be sorted. In the meantime, there are, of course, no categories, or classes, or pigeonholes in nature. We just say there are categories. This is mainly very intelligent of us, or at any rate it can be, but only if we do not forget what we are up to when we do it. We are saying, perhaps, that there are left-handed people and right-handed people, and so we hustle about pasting one or the other of these two labels on everybody we can lay hands on. But then things begin to happen that we didn't intend.

For one thing, the Right-handers begin to spell their name with a capital R. Then one of the more enterprising chaps among them calls a meeting for the purpose of organizing the Right-handers' Mutual Advantage Society. Several curious souls come to the meeting, declare the RMAS to be, as of this day, in existence, elect the enterprising chap its President, and pass a rule that no left-handers may belong to the organization. The President then delivers a Presidential Address in which he points out, between bursts of applause, that there are many more Right-handers than left-handers in the world, and so, he thunders, "We are better than they are!" In fact, he goes on to convince himself and all his other listeners that there is just no comparison at all between Right-handers and left-handers. For one thing, he explains, left-handers don't even prefer to use the right hand. As soon as he points this out it is, of course, perfectly obvious to everyone. And, "as everyone can see," this means that the left-handers are inferior. And if they are inferior, well then, they are inferior.

"And you know about people who are inferior," the President loudly reminds them. "Naturally, we don't want any of those inferior left-handers ringing our bells and saying our prayers and using our salt shakers. If we should ever allow them to do these things, naturally they would get the idea that they were as good as we are, and then they would start presuming to leave their inferior footprints on our superior welcome mats. Do we want that to happen? No! But if we are not alert in defense of our rights and our honor, it is going to happen! Are we going to stand for that? I say No! A thousand times No! Every red-blooded Right-hander among us will take up arms in proud defense of the Right-handers' Mutual Advantage Society and fight on gloriously until the very last left-handed son of the devil has died or surrendered! To arms! Down with the dirty left-handers!"

He is clearly a great leader, a true RMAS hero, and all the Right-handers follow him with fervent devotion, shouting, "To arms! To arms! Down with the dirty left-handers!"

A classification, that is, turns out to be much less simple than it looks at first. There is always the possibility that it will get completely out of hand.

In the beginning it is usually based on something more or less sensible. It may be observed, for example, that people differ with respect to some characteristic or other, such as handedness—or color of skin. There is no question about it, they differ. And so they can be sorted more or less neatly or roughly into groups: the "white," the "black," the "brown," the "red," the "pink," etc. Once the sorting gets under way the most important thing that happens is that individual persons get split off from each other and wind up in quite separate groups.

Then the members of each group start making comparisons. One comparison suggests another and another, until what began as just a little superficial difference in complexion comes to be thought of by all concerned as a big difference involving very nearly all sorts of things. Each group is looked upon as possessing a large and distinctive set of characteristics, physical, mental, moral, political, artistic—not just color. This having come to be, there is a further bit of arresting development to be witnessed: Each new individual, upon being classified as belonging to a group, is immediately taken to be a person who possesses the alleged characteristics of that particular group. It has every appearance of a magical transformation. Just as soon as we say that something is a gillig we start to treat it as though it were a gillig, because any gillig is a gillig. A is A. A rose is a rose. Professor equals Professor equals Professor. Business is business, boys will be boys, and once a Kappa always a Kappa.

So it is that a category ends up meaning much more in general and far less in particular than it starts out to mean. It follows that when we speak about categories we almost always seem to say a great deal more than we can make clear. We might—many people do—say things like this: "The Youth of America believe that Management and Labor should work together to help Business, and to safeguard the Consumer, support the Farmer, rehabilitate the Underprivileged, and relieve the Taxpayer." This is the stuff of which political party platforms are made. And commencement speeches. It is a blowing of verbal bubbles.

It cannot be said too often: Logic is a fine thing. It is the things we do with it that are so alarming.

For most ordinary purposes the main trouble we have with logic—and we have a fantastic amount of trouble with it—is not due to logic itself, but to the fact that it is so much easier to be logical than it is to be sensible. And feeling that we are being logical, we suffer from the illusion that we are necessarily being sensible at the same time. It is a reason for abundant misfortune that we so often behave as though it were not true that in order to be fair and intelligent we have to use something more than logic.

To be logical is easy and it can be exciting too, and fascinating beyond prudent expectation. We can very well say, for example, if we feel for any reason that we should, that there are gilligs, and that for all gilligs it is the case that a gillig is red. That is, it is to be taken as true that all gilligs are red. This we can say. Now, the statement that all gilligs are red we shall take to be true by definition, just as we take as true by definition the statement that all gremlins are little people. It doesn't matter that no one has ever seen a gremlin. We just say there are gremlins, and we just say that they are little people. There need be nothing more to it than that. And so we may just say that there are gilligs and that all gilligs are red.

While we are at it, of course, we may want to say also that all gilligs are round, and soft too, and gormissible as well. And if we say all this we shall have made a major premise: All gilligs are red, round, soft and gormissible.

Next, we may state as our minor premise that all kimmicks are gilligs. Having agreed that this is true by definition, we should have only to find a kimmick. This we may do, of course, without budging an inch—unless we want actually to put our hands on a kimmick, and for us to be logical this is certainly not necessary. We may stay seated quite comfortably and proceed by saying, "Suppose we were to find something." It would, of course, have to be a kimmick or else not be a kimmick. According to the law of the excluded middle it would have to be one or the other, and according to the law of non-contradiction it could not be both. And so, should we suppose that what we had found was a kimmick, then, since all kimmicks are gilligs, and since all gilligs are red, round, soft and gormissible, our conclusion would necessarily be, "This thing is red, round, soft and gormissible."

It is all as simple as saying, for example, "All fish are edible. Trout are fish. Trout are edible." Or, "All the mice in Boston prefer rye bread. This mouse is in Boston. This mouse prefers rye bread."

Nor is all this quite pointless. By no means. Should anyone ever tell you that he has seen a kimmick, you can say, "Ah hah! Not a red one by any chance?"

And the other one will, of course, reply, "It was to be sure! But how did you know?"

"It was a round kimmick?" you will venture.

"Round as any kimmick ever I've seen!" the other one will agree.

Then you can say, "And was it a soft one?"

The other one will surely answer, "How now! You saw it too!"

To which you will reply calmly, "No, as a matter of fact, I didn't. But I have a feeling that it was not only red and round and soft, but gormissible too."

"Gormissible it was!" the other one will gasp, eying you unsteadily.

In logic lurks wizardry for sure.

One thing is to be kept in mind, of course: It might be that there aren't any gilligs, nor any kimmicks. If there aren't, or if there might not necessarily be any, then it is ever so important to allow for this. If you do allow for it you may someday come to be a sensitive poet, beloved by all the world's children and grownups as the ingenious creator of all the delightful red and green and soft and firm and round and square and gormissible and mummable kimmicks and ever so many other adorable gilligs too. What fun they would be! Such jolly verses! And the perfectly lovely illustrations!

Or, allowing for the fact that there aren't any gilligs, or that there are not necessarily any, you may someday come to be a great scientist, author of the famed gilligar theory. As a scientist you will say, "Let us assume that there are gilligs —and let us not be concerned about whether there actually are such things." This sounds very whimsical, if not even a little rash. But there would be method in your scientific madness. For example, it could be that, being the well-known Man from Mars, you were quite puzzled one morning to discover that a glass in which you had been interested was empty. You had been interested in it because you had filled it with water and placed it on your window sill to sun-treat it for several days. You had been accustomed to doing this to water before drinking it. On Mars it was simply the thing to do.

Finding the glass empty, you had no way to understand what had happened to the water. Had the pigeons or squirrels drunk it? Obviously not, since you had placed the glass in your wire-mesh sunner. Even on Mars there were pigeons and squirrels to be kept out of water that was being sun-treated, and sunners kept them out of it. Had the glass tipped? Out of the question. Glasses in sunners can't possibly tip. Had the maid drunk it? She swore she had not, and she was an absolutely honest maid.

Well, then, there was nothing for it but to use your imagination. And so you said, "Let us assume that there is more to water than meets the eye. It could be, for example, that it is made up of exceedingly tiny bits. They would have to be extremely small, and so one glass would hold billions and billions of them. And since our problem is to figure out how the water got out of the glass, let us assume that these tiny pieces of water move frightfully fast, and then it is clear that some of them will be moving very fast as they approach the surface of the water, and before they can be stopped they will have zipped right on past the surface, out of the glass and into the air."

With such a beginning, there is hardly any limit to how imaginative you could become. Besides, bright students would ask questions that could only be answered by assuming that your little bits of water have additional characteristics, until at last they would become very complicated. In fact, they themselves would in due time have to be assumed to be made up of even smaller bits, and these in turn of smaller bits, and so on, and each sized bit would be assumed to have certain characteristics and to move or expand or melt or do something or other in relation to some other sized bit doing something under certain circumstances.

Now, the bits you started with you could call gilligs. You could call those of the next smaller size kimmicks, and the next smaller ones timmits, and so on.

In the course of all this you would have made clear how the water got out of the glass. Before you had finished, moreover, you would have explained rain and dew, the tides, the movements of the oceanic currents, and the circulation of the blood. But you, or some of your brighter students, would also have said things like, "Look, if this is why water disappears from a glass, then, if we assume that there are gilligs everywhere in everything, maybe that will help to explain why bits of paper stick to a comb sometimes." And so electricity and all the things that can be done with it would have come to be understood. The electric light would have been invented, and the wireless, and finally the gillig would have been split and found to be a Pandora's box filled with the undreamed dreams of all the ages.

Finally, someone would be sure to ask you, "But are there *really* gilligs?"

And as a scientist you would reply simply, but very wisely, "We must never forget where gilligs came from in the first place: We have imagined them. And although it is conceivable that there exists some sort of things more or less like what we imagine, yet the fact is that gilligs, as we have imagined them, are much too tiny ever to be seen. Since gilligs, as we have defined them, cannot be seen, there is no point in asking whether we might ever see them. Since this means there is no way to tell for sure and all whether there really are gilligs, there can be no sense in asking whether there are."

In the meantime, by assuming that there are gilligs, you would be able to use your imagination in such ways as to think of practical as well as theoretical possibilities, and to try them out, with effects otherwise impossible or at least highly unlikely.

From all this it is quite clear what scientific theories are. They are symbolic harnesses which we use to hitch our dreams to facts.

Well—of course, then, there are not necessarily any gilligs, nor are gilligs to be necessarily rejected. As children of the mind they sing and dance our most exhilarating hymns of freedom. Meanwhile, presented in a spirit of factual inquiry, the question of whether there really are gilligs may be taken, indeed, to be essentially meaningless—and if you don't allow for this you are rather more than likely to become someday either an enigmatic seer or a mystical skeptic. If you become an enigmatic seer you will testify deviously, though with fervor, that there are gilligs. If you become a mystical skeptic you will assert, with the startling forthrightness of an oracle, that gilligs do not exist. In either case you will attract, as though you were a sounding gong, those who agree with you, and they will generously feed your defiance of all those others who find your convictions outrageous.

But again, and still again, we must remind ourselves that logic is a fine thing. Without it, it is as difficult to be intelligent as it is to be stupid.

And this we may view with wonder all our lives, knowing that all we gain from wonder by wonder is increased.

. . . logic is a fine thing. Without it, it is as difficult to be intelligent as it is to be stupid.

CHAPTER FOURTEEN

Notions Our Language
Puts in Our Heads

✳ It is not only true that the language we use puts words in our mouths; it also puts notions in our heads. This is a way of saying, first of all, that our language consists of a limited number and variety of words. These we do not use willy-nilly, but according to certain rules. Employing these rules, we arrange our words only in certain ways. Arranging words in these ways, we make only certain kinds of statements. Making only such statements, we create truth, in notable measure, in the image of our language.

Our words and our rules for using them make up our language. With this language, there are two major kinds of statements that we make about the world. We make statements about what there is and what it is like; and we make other statements about the places where we find it, the company it keeps, its relationships to other things. In short, we make statements about what there is and statements about what goes with what. Our language identifies individual things or particular experiences, and it relates them to each other in certain ways. In a manner of speaking, we make lists and we draw diagrams. We enumerate things and arrange them. We compile and sort. We assemble and order. We deal with pieces and patterns. In general, we make statements about facts and other statements about the relationships among these facts.

With these basic types of statement in the focus of attention, we are continuing our examination of Stage 4 in the process of communication diagrammed in Figure 1. It is at this stage, we may recall, that the pre-verbal physiological events at Stage 3 come to be transformed into words and other symbols. In order for this most extraordinary transformation to occur there must be a store of symbols and a set of rules for their use—patterns for their arrangement. We have so far examined some of the symbols—speech sounds and letters and words—that make up our language, and we have reviewed some of the facts about our use of words, as such. We have also taken a brief look at the peculiarly fundamental patterns for using words that are provided by our traditional rules of logic, by means of which we fashion the kind of truth we call formal. We also call it truth by convention—the kind of truth that consists of the rules of the game of language which, by common agreement and general consent, we all follow as best we can. Now, we are about to consider how important a role these patterns of formal truth, these rules of the game of language, play in our fashioning of another kind of truth—factual or empirical truth, the truth, as we take it to be, about the world and our experiences in it.

Logic, as we have previously remarked more than once, is a fine thing—it is the mistakes we make in trying to be logical that are so disturbing. One of the most common and serious of these mistakes is that of confusing formal truth with factual truth. It is possible to stay fairly clear of this confusion by keeping in mind that formal truths are rules for the use of words or other symbols. This means they are definitions, since any definition is a rule for the use of a word. We can make up new definitions, and there is a possibility that they might be just as good or useful as they would be had we found them ready-made in a standard dictionary. After all, the ones we do find in the dictionary were once newly made. They were somebody's inventions of a sort, just as new words are inventions. A dictionary, after all, is a kind of catalog of symbolic inventions. Well, the point is that a definition—which is a formal truth, a rule, or regulation—is not to be mistaken for a factual proposition. It is not a statement about the non-verbal world of fact and experience. It is words about words.

So now we are going to talk about words that are not about words. We are going to talk about words that are about experiences and facts of a non-verbal sort. Nothing elaborate—although this sort of thing could be spun out into a very intricate verbal filigree of analysis and theorizing. What is to follow will be restricted for the most part, as a matter of fact, to making just one point.

This one point is that what we say about the world is not wholly determined by how clever we are, how high our

IQ's may be, and how much knowledge about the world we possess. It is determined also, and to a major degree, by the ways in which we arrange the words at our disposal. And when we pause long enough to think about it with some care, we have to end up realizing that we customarily employ very few ways of arranging words.

In order to come at this very fundamental problem as effectively as possible, let us talk about you, and see what sorts of words we use and how we arrange them. But let us try to say things that are important. Such as: You are lovely.

I suggest we not quibble just now over the meaning of *you*—and that we not be simple-minded enough either to suppose that it has a simple meaning. What it means is even much more complex than it was made out to be by William James, intellectually dapper father of American psychology, who pointed out that each one of us has many selves: The one known to our employers, the one known to our customers or clients, the self of our family circle, the one who shows up at church on Sundays, the self who appears or explodes at club conventions, et cetera. This list is barely a beginning. The fact is that you have as many selves as there are persons who know you. More than that: You have, or are, as many selves as there are occasions when people, including yourself, react to you. And, to paraphrase Lincoln, you can't be lovely to all the people all the time. The statement that you are lovely is considerably unclear, unless we know who makes it and under what conditions.

But let us acknowledge all this, and then be reasonable and not fuss over it, not now, that is. You are lovely—one of you, at least, and in the opinion of at least one person, even if that one person is you, and if only for one moment. So, all right, suppose we see what the rest of the sentence says. And we ought not overlook the fact that this simple arrangement of words consists of a pronoun and an adjective joined by a verb.

It will help to give a name to this kind of sentence, make it easier to talk about it, and easier to divine what it says. We usually call it a subject-predicate form of sentence. It is a sentence that says something about a subject; in this case the subject is *you*. What it says about you is a predicate. That is, *lovely* is a predicate. And the little word *are* is a verb of predication. It relates a subject and a predicate. In this case it stands for a relationship between *you* and *lovely*. What sort of relationship is this?

The *are* seems to indicate that the loveliness is inside you, that you are what is being lovely. This means that the loveliness is related to you by being within you, or a part of you. And so, with these three little words, and with our customary rules for putting them together, we put the following idea into our heads: There is a thing that is a loveliness and there is a thing that is a you, and the loveliness is inside the you.

There is a possibility that there may be nothing wrong with this—but, of course, it makes all the difference in the world who is talking. When I say *you,* I am referring to you as I see you, know you, like you, hate you, compare you with other persons, sympathize with you, misunderstand you, and so on and on. This means that the word *you,* when I use it, refers partly to me (Stages 2, 3, 4 and 5 of Figure 1) and partly to you (Stage 1). Where, then, is the loveliness? We could succumb to the intriguing influence of Gertrude Stein and say that the loveliness is in the you that is in me. That could be a useful way to put it, but it is not the way we usually talk about such things, and when we say something in a very unusual way most people are more impressed by the fact that it "sounds funny" than they are by the sense it makes.

Meanwhile, it seems clear enough that the word *you* refers necessarily to something that is a joint product of you and me. If we look at Figure 1 again, we see that you are represented at Stage 1 and the reacting, evaluating and speaking that I am doing are represented at Stages 2, 3, 4 and 5, and the word *you* necessarily refers to all these and not just to whatever there may be at Stage 1. One way to put it is to say that the word *you* stands for some sort of relationship between you and me, a relationship in which I observe, react to, judge, abstract, and finally symbolize you in words. And so another way to sum it up is to say that the word *you* refers to an abstraction—and it is my abstraction of you.

"You are lovely" becomes, then, "My abstraction of you is to me lovely." Where does that leave the loveliness? Inside me, apparently. In other words, the way you look to me and the way I feel about you when I look at you make me want to say that something is lovely, and since I don't understand what is going on I make the mistake of supposing it is you that is lovely. This would seem to be meanwhile an understandable mistake, since I am looking at you and thinking about you when I have the feeling inside me that makes something seem so lovely. If I were more aware of my abstracting and evaluating and projecting processes, I would say simply and quite accurately, "Looking at you gives me a feeling that I call lovely."

The mistake I make is all the more understandable in view of the fact that the language I learned on my mother's knee is such that just about the most common or "natural" sort of thing to say under the circumstances is something like, "You are lovely." This is a particular form of arranging words, the subject-predicate form, which I have learned very well, just as you have, and everyone else who speaks our daily language. Probably not one in a million would say, "Looking at you gives me a feeling I call lovely"—and realize that this was radically different in meaning from, "You are lovely." It would take a person far more conscious of his own language functions than most of us are to see clearly that one of these sentences says the loveliness is in you and the other one says it is in me. And that makes the two sentences very, very different.

Generally speaking, the trouble with the subject-predicate form of sentence is that it seems to make out that the speaker is talking solely about the world outside himself (Stage 1) when, as a matter of fact, he is talking about the goings-on inside himself (Stages 2-5). The goings-on inside the speaker may be influenced more or less, of course, by the world outside; but whatever the world outside may be like independently of the speaker, the knowledge and understanding he has of it are necessarily affected considerably by being filtered through his own abstracting and evaluating and symbolizing nervous system. Now, all this is about as important as anything could possibly be to anyone even the least bit interested in talking sense, in being a dependable speaker, in not fooling anyone—including oneself.

If our language puts words in our mouths and the forms of our language put ideas in our heads, and if these turn out to be confusing words and distorting ideas, that would seem to be worth our attention. Probably the most important thing to be done about it is to check our impressions against those of other people, so that when we say something like, "You are lovely," we have at least a rough idea of how well others agree with us. An obvious way to do this is to say to these other people, "To me Gwendolyn seems lovely. Does she seem lovely to you?" If they say she does, you can say simply, "Gwendolyn is lovely," and you won't get into trouble, at least not with these other people who agree with you. You are not likely to start any unpleasant arguments, and the other people probably will not think you are queer. They will think you are right and so you will think they are right, and when people feel this way about each other— well, they don't learn much from each other but they do tend to get along rather nicely. What all this means is that the subject-predicate form of statement works quite well so long as the listener agrees with the speaker to begin with. In fact, it seems to intensify their agreement, to make them feel closer together than before one of them said something which the other found congenial. "You took the words right out of my mouth" can signal an intensification of friendship.

But when the listener does not agree with the speaker to begin with, when in fact they differ considerably in their abstractions (Stages 2-5 and 2'-5' respectively), then a subject-predicate remark like "Gwendolyn is lovely" has the effect of making them all the more aware of the fact that they differ from each other. And if they try to keep on talking under these circumstances they are quite likely to repel each other increasingly, expressing their disagreement in ever more clear and decisive ways until they may even come to blows, or physically escape from each other's "stupidity" and "stubbornness," or work themselves into a kind of semantic clinch in which they maintain an oppressively polite estrangement.

"Gwendolyn is lovely," you say.

"Gwendolyn? Lovely? That caved-in . . . Now, see here, if you say she's lovely you're just crazy, that's all."

"Who's crazy? You're the one who's crazy!"

And so two persons, starting out by taking thoughtlessly and falsely for granted that they are both talking about a fact quite outside themselves, end up saying things about themselves that sound for all the world as though they were talking very pointedly about each other. This taxes severely their capacities for good will and friendship, with consequences as fruitless as they are unpleasant.

All of which would be quite unthinkable had both persons been trained to understand the basic fact that what we say is determined largely by the patterns or forms we use, quite unconsciously as a rule, for arranging words.

What we have just observed about the form of the sentence, "You are lovely," is also to be observed about such other sentences as these:

Greek culture was noble and good.

The Brooklyn Dodgers are excruciating.

Wealth is evil.

Money is marvelous.

It is to be observed, in fact, about most of the statements we make. It holds for any of our subject-predicate sentences, and a large proportion of the sentences we make are of this type. And we should add to these another very common form of statement in which *is, are, am,* or some other form of the verb *to be,* is used to join one noun with another, as in the sentence, "Dishonesty is a sin." This amounts to saying that dishonesty equals sin, or dishonesty is the same as sin. We may call this a statement of identification. And we usefully refer to the *is* (or other form of *to be*) in such a sentence as an *is* of identification. Whereas such an *is* joins a noun with another noun, an *is* of predication joins a noun with an adjective. The two, the *is* of identification and the *is* of predication, have much the same effect, as a rule. After all, "Dishonesty is a sin" can also be put in the form, "Dishonesty is sinful." For practically everyone no doubt the two sentences would mean the "same" thing and have the "same" effect.

A further word, however, is to be said especially about the *is* of identification. When we say, for example, "Man is an animal," we may insist that we do not mean to identify man as an animal, to make man out to be the same as other animals. We may say that instead we mean "only" to classify man with all other animals. In other words, we may say that in "Man is an animal" the *is* simply serves the purpose of "class inclusion." That is, it serves to place man within the general class or category of animals. Having said this, however, we might find it just a bit difficult to make clear what we have said. Most of us would not only deny having said that man is exactly the same as all other animals, but we would also deny having said that man is exactly the same as any other animal. Some of us would doubtless take refuge in the claim that we had "merely" said that man is "animal-like." After so much of this quite a few of us would admit frankly that we had simply repeated something we had often heard but which we had never stopped to wonder about very much, and that we really didn't know precisely what we had meant to say.

It is very easy to put something into a class; it is very difficult to make clear just what we have done in doing this. It seems to be generally true, however, that at the very least "class inclusion" serves strongly to emphasize similarities and to minimize differences. The sentence, "Man is an animal," probably suggests to most of us that a man is a good deal like an animal—or like "other animals"—and that this is much more important evidently than the possibility (which the sentence does not express) that a man may be in some ways different from animals.

Perhaps all this can be fairly well summed up for present purposes by saying that in our common language behavior, identification is not usually an all-or-none affair. Stark identification is to be found in some cases in mental hospitals. An occasional patient will indulge now and then in such outright identification of different levels of abstraction, of words with things, as to write the word *meat* on bits of paper and eat the paper. More commonly, such patients identify one person or thing with another, reacting to all nurses, or all doctors, or all fried eggs, respectively, as though they were absolutely the same. But, of course, this is not unheard of outside mental hospitals among so-called ordinary people. There are ever so many persons for whom all Republicans or all Democrats, as the case may be, are indistinguishable— at least in a polling booth—one from another.

For even larger numbers this is true with respect to certain foods; a person who has for any reason acquired a food dislike tends to exercise the dislike absolutely, so that when he says, "I don't eat rhubarb," he means he doesn't eat any rhubarb anywhere any time at all. He means he doesn't touch the stuff. To him one rhubarb is exactly like all other rhubarbs. And this is the way some persons react to Negroes, or Buddhists, or Catholics, or Protestants, or Hebrews, or Mexicans, or millionaires, or shop girls, or abstract paintings, or operas, or professors, or labor leaders, and so forth quite endlessly. It is by no means easy, and it is sometimes impossible, to tell the difference between the examples of such identification to be seen inside mental hospitals and the examples of it to be seen outside the hospitals. Whenever identification is this extreme, whenever it approaches the absolute, it would appear to be pathological no matter where it is seen, or in whom.

Most of us most of the time do not exhibit such extreme forms of identification of different levels of abstraction, of words with things, of inferences with descriptions, or of one thing with other things. We merely "tend to some degree" to identify words with the non-verbal things they might—or might not—stand for, and we "tend to some degree" to treat one member of a class as though he or it were the same as any other member of the same class. "To some degree"—that is, most of us feel there are or may be exceptions, even when we feel convinced that the general rule far outshadows them. Most of us will go only so far in "overlooking" the fact of skin color, creed, or social class of any particular individual, and there comes a point at which we say, "After all, I'm as broad-minded as the next person and I'm just as democratic as anyone else, but when it comes to choosing my sorority sisters—well, after all." In other words, for most of us there is a point beyond which any Slopokian is the same as every other Slopokian. Beyond a certain limit in any instance, we indulge in absolute or very nearly absolute identification—we lose sight of the individual himself and react instead to the class or category in which we have chosen to include him. This is to be remembered whenever we say that most of us only "tend to some degree" to identify words with things and things with each other. And it is to be remembered also whenever we tell ourselves that the *is* of identification is somehow very different from what seems like a far more innocent, even useful and virtuous, *is* of "class inclusion."

Because of the nature of our language it is impossible to avoid predication, identification, and class inclusion. It is not that they are to be avoided. They appear to be essential indeed to what we call our "higher mental processes," to problem solving, to creative thinking, to all that we understand by intelligence and genius, and to the wise conduct of practical affairs. We cannot, so far as we know, carry on the abstracting process without predicating, identifying, and classifying. The issue concerns the fact that when we do these things unknowingly, without a reasonable understanding of the processes they involve, we "tend to some degree" to do them to an extreme degree—and in their most extreme, absolute, and "unconscious" forms they are pathological, and their effects tend to be unjust, confusing, destructive, and generally regrettable. That is, there is likely to be something quite invalid in talking about a category as though it were a single individual—and especially vice versa.

Any statement made about a category—the category "professor," for example—amounts to a definition, and it fits any particular member of the category, any particular professor, for example, only partially at best. It is very useful indeed to distinguish clearly between verbal definitions, which are words about words, and factual statements, which are words about things that are not-words. Definitions are formal truths, and they are not to be mistaken for factual truths.

Skill in making these crucial distinctions is not easily acquired. Its development requires much and constant practice. Our schools do not always prove very helpful in this connection. In fact, it would appear that very few teachers are systematically trained to impart such proficiency as this to children or even to students in colleges and universities. It is especially unfortunate that our neighbors and friends do not seem as a rule to mind or even to notice our failures to use this sort of skill, and so they do not remind us very often of the distinctions we are to make between definitions and propositions, between truth that is formal and truth that is factual, and between the degree to which our statements are about something outside ourselves and the degree to which they are about something inside ourselves—as we saw in the case of the sentence, "You are lovely." Because our friends and neighbors are usually so indifferent to whether we do or don't make these distinctions we seldom suffer social penalties if we fail to make them. There are no four-color ads in magazines warning us of our common semantic equivalents of B.O. and halitosis, and cajoling and frightening us into being careful how we use *is* and how we identify and predicate and classify and project. And so we are mainly on our own, each of us, and we shall continue to be until a considerable number of people take these things seriously and start making them matters of neighborhood gossip.

But, then, perhaps there is reason enough, besides what the neighbors will think of us, for developing habits of semantic cleanliness and grooming. We have discovered, most of us, that quite aside from what other people think, there are pleasures and advantages to be derived from bathing. There is, as well, a compelling satisfaction to be gained from being clear and talking sense, even when no one else may seem to realize that that is what we are doing.

*. . . the more fully aware we are
of the language forms we are using . . .
the more of a say we have
in what we have to say.*

CHAPTER FIFTEEN

The What That Goes with What

✳ Wordless goings-on inside the brain change strangely into sounds of self within the throat. In our struggle to become more fully conscious of this transformation of our silences into our vocal meanings, we have described and contemplated it in terms of "speech sounds," "words," "vocabulary," "logical forms," "formal truth," "factual truth," "subject-predicate sentences," "abstraction," "identification," "predication," "classification," "projection." We have achieved a very important purpose if we have gained, or have had reaffirmed, a clear conviction that here is a mighty expanse of human problems. It is to be stressed that they are *human* problems, and to the degree that we appreciate and understand them, we have a peculiarly good grasp of what it means to be human.

But there are more problems than we have yet considered. Specifically, there are certain kinds of relationships in addition to those we discussed in the last chapter. Some of these are expressed by the common forms of our language—even when the relationships do not correspond to what we are, in fact, trying to describe.

The great bulk of our sentences, for example, seem to express one-way relationships: "John loves Mary"; "Germs cause disease"; "Daddy will fix it." Such sentences make up a very large proportion of those we speak and write. Fortunately most of us have a saving store of unspoken good sense, so that while all we say is that John loves Mary we understand in a vague sort of way, at least, that either Mary loves John, too, or else there is something peculiar about the way he loves her. We know, sometimes but certainly not always, that most relationships do not work only one way, even though we say they do. Every effect is also a cause, every cause an effect. It is an old assumption, admittedly a little rusty from being so seldom used, that everything is related to everything else and that the cause of anything is everything. John Gunther said almost exactly these words in discussing world tensions a few years ago. Others have expressed essentially the same notion in dealing with a great variety of problems and situations. There is in all this a grain of truth that you can hardly ever shake out of your consciousness. Nevertheless, as a rule we are simply bothered by it, made uneasy by the fact that its implications seem to render questionable or even downright unacceptable so many of the things we say. And we say them so easily, so glibly, as though we were some sort of mechanical sound-makers.

Perhaps we are—to a degree far greater than we have been prepared to understand. In *Prescription for Rebellion*

Robert Lindner refers in a startling passage to the mass of men as living "under the dominance of the unconscious to such an extent that they exist after the manner of sleep-walkers." (*Prescription for Rebellion*, by Robert Lindner, New York: Rinehart, 1952, p. 267.) In the vaguely unnerving quality of this figure of speech there is a clue to something in human experience that is evidently far more important than has been realized by the world's physicians and "doctors of souls." This something has been hinted at and obliquely considered by many. Lindner has called it "awareness." Psychoanalysts commonly contrast it with "the unconscious" and poets sing of it as "sensitivity." There was one, the late Alfred Korzybski, who illumined more brightly than most the crucial human quality we are striving to capture. He spoke of it as a consciousness of abstracting and of all that abstracting tends to involve: identification of words and things, of the seeable and the unseeable; projection; overdefinition and underdefinition of terms; the multiordinality of abstracting; and all the rest of what he summarized and organized in that curious three-dimensional diagram of his that he called the structural differential. And all that this represents he referred to engagingly as the consciousness of self that counteracts self-consciousness. (See Alfred Korzybski, *Science and Sanity: An Introduction to Non-aristotelian Systems and General Semantics*. Lancaster, Pa.: Science Press, 1933. Second ed., 1941. Third edition, 1948.) It is to be observed, however, and with chagrin, that in all probability most of us are insufficiently contemplative in our reactions to the printed page to have lingered over Korzybski's unusual wordings long enough either to have rejected them thoughtfully or to have made them our own for good reason.

There is also a growing band of scholars, who trace their intellectual lineage back to Charles Sanders Peirce and Bertrand Russell and Ernst Mach and Ludwig Wittgenstein —men like Tarski, the late Maurice Schlick, Carnap, Ayer, Feigl, Bergmann, Reichenbach, Quine, Charles Morris, and the list grows ever longer—men who are devoted to the problems of meaning and truth, of language and logic, of man's symbols and the extraordinary difficulties, and occasional brilliant successes, men have in trying to talk sense by means of them. These scholars have been variously identified as logical positivists, semanticists, philosophers of science, and so on. They have endeavored mightily to make men aware, at new and significant depths, of the essentials of sense and nonsense, of the many meanings of meaning, and the divers faces of truth. They have succeeded in enriching the *awareness* of at least a few of the highly literate, and if they have not influenced greatly the consciousness of "the celebrated man in the street" (T. C. Mits, as the Liebers call him in their charming book, *The Education of T. C. Mits,* Norton, 1944) there are at least two obvious reasons for this. One is that T. C. Mits is not overly given to reading heavy matter, and the other is that the philosophers of science are not fanatically committed to the ideal of simple English.

What matters more than this, however, is that there is abroad in the world these days a substantial number of groups and individuals whose varied labors make inevitable a deepening sense of self, a more and more effective *awareness,* for all who attend, even for those who attend only a little. Those who follow and extend the trails blazed by Freud and Pavlov, by Russell and Schlick and Korzybski, by such cultural anthropologists as Boas and Sapir, and the other pioneers in the systematic exploration of humanness, are building roads to a future surely to be preferred to the best of our yesterdays. For it would seem certainly to be in man's greater awareness of himself, in his more effective understanding of his own motives and of the actions to which he is driven by them, that man is destined to discover his most constructive possibilities. Preoccupation with the study of man and his behavior, study in the modern scientific and intensive clinical sense, gives us some basis at least for long-range optimism, even though we may be tempted all too often to give way to short-term pessimism. It seems clear that our knowledge is increasing, and there appears to be good reason to hold to the conviction that the more knowledge we possess the better, and most especially is this true when the knowledge is about ourselves.

A particularly useful kind of such knowledge is that which we are examining, knowledge of our symbolic processes. In spite of the fact, as we were just now considering, that in a wordless kind of way we understand that most relationships among the facts of our experience are complex, we usually say—because the prevailing forms of our language say it for us—that one thing affects another, that A affects B, as though B did not also affect A. In the meantime, A and B interact in practically all instances. The way we feel affects what and how much we eat and what and how much we eat affect how we feel. Action leads to reaction as dependably as the sun rides the heavens day after day. We take for granted that structure determines function, but the biceps of any weight-lifter are arresting evidence of the effect that function has on structure. The thought affects the thinker. And the poet Yeats etched it memorably: "How can we tell the dancer from the dance?"

There is still more that is wrong with saying that A causes B. Such a statement fails, for example, to mention the many other factors or forces besides A that contribute in one way or another—and all together—to the causing of B. It is not enough to say simply that germs cause disease. They don't always. Children from broken homes are not always delinquent. Sparing the rod—or not sparing it—does not inevitably spoil the child. And people who are given sufficient money for their needs do not always lose their incentive for work. There is evidently not just one cause, even in a single case, of allergy, or tooth decay, arthritis, an inferiority complex, retarded speech development and most of the other deterrents to human serenity.

There is a technical term specifically used to refer to overly simple one-factor statements of causation. Such statements are said to be elementalistic. They point to single elements as causes of events which, on closer scrutiny, are seen to be the outcomes of many elements, working not singly but in relationship to each other. Elementalistic statements deny that everything is the cause of anything; in their most extreme forms they reverse this sentiment, making out that some one thing is responsible for everything—or all of something: money is the root of all evil; what this country needs is a good five-cent cigar; and early to bed and early to rise makes a man healthy and wealthy and wise.

It is often the case that when we speak about causes we are talking, as a matter of fact, about correlations. Two things are correlated when they "go together." For example, height is to a certain degree correlated with weight, which means that tall individuals tend to be heavier than short ones. Now, no one would say that height *causes* weight. It is simply that they are correlated: co-related, meaning generally that to some degree they vary together, the more of one the more of the other, or the less of one the less of the other. This, of course, is positive correlation. There are negative correlations, too. Size of family tends to be negatively correlated to some degree with socioeconomic level of family, which means roughly that married couples who have very little money and schooling tend to have more children than do those who have considerable wealth and education. This is a case of the more of A the less of B, a negative co-relation.

Co-relation can be one or the other of at least three different kinds of relationship. It can be the kind we call coincidence. A and B can vary together and yet be quite unrelated to each other. For many years the world population has been increasing, and during this time all sorts of other things as well have been increasing, or decreasing, but many of them have not varied specifically because of the up-trend in the earth's population. It is not obvious at least that recent changes in the proportion of men who use electric razors, or the percentage who wear vests, or the proportion of women who smoke cigarettes are related, except by coincidence, to population trends.

A correlation between A and B can mean that both are being affected by a third factor. High-school students who smoke cigarettes may make lower marks than those who don't, not necessarily, or not only, because smoking causes lower marks, but because the students' psychological reasons for smoking may be the same reasons why they do not work at their studies more effectively.

Finally, if changes in A are correlated with changes in B it can mean that the two are to some degree related in a cause-and-effect or action-and-reaction sense. For example, the positive correlation between body weight and amount of food eaten—more exactly, caloric intake—would seem to be a reasonably clear case in point. Even in this case, however, the relationship is not a simple one—and it illustrates the general rule that such relationships seldom are simple. For some persons weight seems to be very responsive to amount of caloric intake, while for others apparently it is much less so. Some individuals appear to be able to lose weight more easily than others are. The correlation between caloric intake and weight gain or loss seems not to tell the whole story. There are many other factors involved, not only metabolic and biochemical but also psychological. But the correlation does seem to tell part of the story. The test is to keep everything else just as it is, or was, so far as possible, and vary the caloric intake. This would be an experimental check of the correlation, and if the check were to show that, with the other known variables relatively unchanged, increase and decrease in amount of food consumed (caloric intake) were followed by corresponding increase and decrease in body weight, x pounds for y calories as dependably as clockwork, there would be good reason to conclude that this was no mere coincidence, and that it was not a case of some indirect relationship acting through one or more other factors.

The notion of correlation is fundamental in the thinking of scientific investigators. It is plainly an important step beyond the more crude and frequently beclouding and misleading idea of cause, as most of us use it most of the time. Often when we say that A causes B, a scientist would prefer to say, more carefully, that A goes with B, or A and B occur together, or changes in A are systematically associated with changes in B. He will say that A causes B—or. more precisely, A tends with a certain degree of consistency to be followed by B—only after he has determined, under adequately controlled conditions, that this is, in fact, the case. The point to be stressed is that this more careful and effective way of using language requires a good deal of special training and knowledge, and not a little self-discipline. Ordinary language, employed in our ordinary ways, does a much more fuzzy job of thinking for us.

Much that is of the greatest significance to us in all this business about the ways we talk about—and the ways we understand—relationships is to be pointed up especially in connection with what we may call self-reflexive relationships. These involve a kind of recoil or feedback, as seen in the effects on the thinker of his own thoughts, on the observer of his own observations, on the dreamer of his own dreaming—and, remembering Yeats, the effects on the dancer of the dance.

We refer to a particularly important kind of self-reflexive relationship when we point to the fact, as we have so many times in this book, that any speaker is his own listener, often his own most responsive and vulnerable listener. Our common language tends strongly to obscure this fact. It is only by taking special pains—by carrying out a personal language reform, no less—that one can talk about it in anything like an effective fashion. In our usual way we talk about the speaker and the listener as though they were two different persons, not as though they were one and the same individual. It is not to be missed nor passed over lightly that in English we have no word for a-speaker-listening-to-and-being-affected-by-and-responding-to-himself. About the nearest we ever come to referring to this universally occurring and impressively ignored phenomenon is found in the phrase that only partially covers it: a man talking to himself. It is not only important that there are self-reflexive relationships such as this, but it is also important that we find it so very difficult to talk about them. The things we find difficult to talk about we find correspondingly difficult to attend to in any way at all, even to notice when they are all around us. The point is underscored by Molière's newly rich fellow who was amazed to learn from his social tutor that everything written or spoken is either poetry or prose, and so—lo and behold—he had been speaking prose all his life without knowing it!

As we become more and more aware of the fact that most relationships with which we have to deal are self-reflexive and non-elementalistic, we are forcibly struck by the enormity of the evident error in our traditional teaching, in school and out. The great bulk of our teaching prepares children to think and act as though either they do unto others or are done unto by them, any given thing is either a cause or an effect, causes as well as effects are usually singular, and so on. So trained, they approach situation after situation with the best of intentions and with good common sense—as we understand common sense—but with assumptions and responses that are decidedly inappropriate. With but rare and partial exceptions we ourselves were so trained as children, and as a consequence we are trying as adults to deal with our personal and social problems as though they were far more simple than they are, and by so doing we end up making them much more complicated than they need be.

In recent years, however, new developments have served to quicken our consciousness of these matters. Such books as Hayakawa's *Language in Thought and Action,* Wiener's *The Human Use of Human Beings,* Rapoport's *Science and the Goals of Man* as well as his *Operational Philosophy,* Chase's *The Power of Words,* Reichenbach's *The Rise of Scientific Philosophy* and a growing number of other books more or less like these are engaging the thoughtful attention of increasing numbers of readers, Moreover, research having to do with electronic servomechanisms is forcing itself increasingly upon the public consciousness, not only because "mechanical brains" are used in the public glare of television to tally national elections, but also because the growing automation of industry made possible by servomechanisms threatens—or promises—drastic changes in our economic way of life.

The effects of our new knowledge of feedback processes and automation principles are to be seen particularly in research and development in the broad field of communication. A curious and very significant side light on this is to be noted in the fact that, just as the invention of the telephone was followed by the development of our commonly accepted "telephonic" theory of the human nervous system in which the brain is likened to a telephone central switchboard, today the servomechanism is being used by more and more neurologists and psychologists as a theoretical model for purposes of explaining our neural functions. The cybernetic or self-adjusting control mechanisms of the human brain are the subject of a great deal of engrossing speculation. Some of the more important and exciting discussion of this sort is to be found in a slender volume, *Doubt and Certainty in Science,* by the British anatomist, J. Z. Young.

Feedback processes provide striking examples of self-reflexiveness and self-reflexive relationships. A fairly practical way to approach this problem is to recognize two general kinds of feedback. Stated with reference to a person speaking, these may be indicated by saying that one comes from sources inside the speaker himself, internal feedback, and the other comes from sources outside the speaker, external feedback. Put very simply, internal feedback is at play in the speaker who is being reflective about something he has just said, while external feedback is operating when the speaker is being sensitive to the reactions of other people to what he has said. When external feedback is at work it necessarily affects—and is affected by—the internal feedback that is going on at the same time. The two kinds are doubtless even more closely interwoven than this would indicate, however: even if no other persons are present, the reflecting that it done by a speaker or thinker on what he has just said or thought is influenced in some degree by his past experiences—and his contemplations of future experiences—with external feedback. So, when we say that there are two kinds of feedback we do so with the realization, of course, that while they might be distinguished, one from the other, they cannot possibly be disentangled. As his own listener, every speaker attends as best he can as though with the ears of a multitude.

The importance of all this to each of us arises particularly from the fact that in our attempts to talk about reality we do two things with language, as we have previously observed. We point verbally to individual facts, we identify them, we tell them apart, we sort and group them. And having done this, we arrange and organize them; we make statements about the relationships among them. The kinds of relationship we tend to traffic in most of the time are simple, constant, one-way, one-factor or elementalistic relationships. In the meantime "what there are there" to be observed and experienced are mostly complex, varying, many-factored, interacting, self-reflexive co-relationships. Gearing ourselves to reality appears to be in large measure a matter of becoming more and more sensitive to such relationships, more adroit in recognizing them, and more effective in talking and thinking about them. And this is particularly important so far as they affect ourselves. The keening up of this sort of sensitivity may be accomplished in more than one way, of course, but certainly it is enhanced by thinking as clearly, and imaginatively, as we can about the processes responsible for the language that does so much of our thinking for us. For the more we do this the more freedom we come by, freedom *from* what Stuart Chase recognized as the tyranny of words, freedom *to* evaluate our own evaluations and so self-reflexively to work our way, however slowly, toward the higher reaches of what we might have been.

In all this our concern is with Stage 4 in the communication process diagramed in Figure 1. This is the stage of fateful transformation—where the wordless goings-on inside the tissues of the brain become, as if by magic, the sounds of self within the throat. These sounds of self are expressed at Stage 5. We have been at pains to point up the role played by our conventional and habitual language forms in determining at Stage 4 the particular verbalizations we make in trying to turn our experiences into words. These language forms favor the expression of certain kinds of relations among facts, and between the speaker and what he is talking about—as well as certain kinds of relations between the speaker and his speech. The more automatically or thoughtlessly we employ the forms of our language, the more thoroughly and automatically they determine the thoughts we have and the statements we make. It follows that the more fully aware we are of the language forms we are using, and the kinds of relationships we are representing and stressing, the more of a say we have in what we have to say.

The difference this makes is reflected in a deeply important sense in our feelings and attitudes, our persistent motivations and evaluational tendencies—and in the conflicts among these. To the extent that our language does a kind of thinking for us that disregards the reality of sense, we grow more or less accustomed to a sort of dreamy, sleepwalkerish state in which we can be readily moved to fear and worry, discouragement and resentment, and other distracting and disabling evaluations. On the other hand, as practically every elementary textbook in psychiatry emphasizes, so long as we take reality into account, seeing reasonably clearly what stares us in the face, and doing a kind of evaluating that takes sensed reality for its starting base and its testing ground, we are far less likely to give way to anxieties, intense or persistent hostilities, or other so-called emotional disturbances. So-called because what we call our "emotions" cannot be disengaged—except in a disembodied verbal sense —from what we call our "thoughts." Our manner of evaluating determines importantly not only our insights but also our feelings. Indeed, the sorts of reactions we recognize as overly emotional in some undesirable way turn out almost always to be examples of poor evaluating, or the consequences of poor evaluating. As a matter of fact, there are advantages in using more freely than we do the word "evaluation" at those times when we would otherwise feel driven to choose between the terms "emotion" and "thought," because whatever on non-verbal levels we might possibly mean by the dividing line between "emotion" and "thought" is necessarily arbitrary. The attempt to make an extensional distinction between these two terms, if pushed very far, tends to result in statements that are whimsical, vague, clearly false, or simply meaningless.

The main point is that at Stage 4, we may usefully assume, we find our persistent, basic, or characteristic feelings, attitudes, evaluational habits, and motivations, and these appear to affect and to be affected by the wordings we use in symbolizing our silent inner states. So it is that at Stage 5 we say the things we do, influenced not only by the "facts" we are talking about and by the vocabularies and the language forms at our command, not only by our levels of intelligence and our funds of information, but also by our feelings, moods, sentiments, prejudices, loves, antagonisms, dreads—and all the conflicts in which they are embroiled.

In this light, certain it is that every speaker talks not only to himself but also from within himself and unavoidably about himself. He may at the same time refer, in greater or lesser degree, and more or less clearly, to the world that exists, at Stage 1 as we suppose, independently of his symbol system and the uses he makes of it. Nevertheless, the verbal representation of this world which the speaker produces at Stage 5 must necessarily have been filtered through Stages 2, 3, and 4 inside his own skin. The facts in the world outside, as we have said before in discussing the process of abstracting, are strained or filtered by us through our eyes and nerves and brain tissues, and they surrender their independent character to the resulting state of affairs inside the nervous system with which they become enmeshed.

It is this internal state of affairs, not the events outside the nervous system, that we transform into words or other symbols.

And so it is, necessarily so, that every speaker speaks only for himself and not for nature, only of the things he perceives and supposes and not of the things that may otherwise be.

By way of a living awareness of this necessity, and a sensitivity to the wondrous transition from silence into symbol, we may come in time upon our good hope of freedom from the Truth that distracts us from the truths there are to know.

*Sound is so much with us that we perform
the wonder of listening with very nearly
the innocence of the beasties afield.*

CHAPTER SIXTEEN

The Words Whose Wings Are Broken

✳ In the last eight chapters we have been examining what goes on when one person says something to someone else, or when a speaker is his own listener. We made a diagram of the series of stages through which this process moves in its ever-wonderful transitions, and up to now we have considered the first four of these stages. As we have noted, they involve, in order: (1) some event or happening external to the individual's eyes, ears, or other sensory "receiving stations"; (2) sensory stimulation; (3) a state of affairs inside the nervous system that is a joint product of the newly arrived impulses of stimulation and the goings-on in progress at the time of their arrival; and (4) the transformation of this silent, or non-verbal, state of affairs inside the person's nervous system into words or other symbols.

181

This last stage seems particularly complicated and we have given over the past five chapters to an exploration of its various facets and involutions. During this stage the symbol systems available to the person, together with his knowledge, beliefs, purposes, attitudes and feelings, operate to bring about whatever it is that gets said finally at Stage 5. What does get said, of course, is usually a far and faint cry from what might have got said. For Stage 4 would seem to be something like a moving picture production studio, with a great deal of censoring and revising, and cutting and patching going on, and with far more being felt, thought of and tried out than finally meets the eye—or ear. And just as the final production of a movie studio is limited in form by what can be done with cameras, film and projectors—and censors—so the final symbolic production of the human speaker is limited by what can be done with his receiving apparatus, his available language forms and symbolization processes, and his projection mechanism—and the cultural taboos by which he is affected. Very important also is the speaker's degree of awareness of all this and of the hazards as well as the beneficent wonders entailed in its use.

At Stage 5 the final draft is issued. Up to this point we have been concerned with the drafting of it, and we have been interested mainly in the patterns of sounds and words that enter into it, and in "what they say." Now we are concerned with how the final draft is issued, how it gets said, the means used to deliver it to the listener or receiver.

So it comes about that we are now ready to have a look at Stage 5 of the communication process, at what goes on and what sometimes goes wrong at this stage. And we shall restrict our considerations to speech, rather than writing, architecture, or the dance, for example, because by doing this we can view more clearly what is fundamental.

Primarily what happens at Stage 5 is that words get spoken. And what happens to the words that get spoken is that they become sound waves and light waves. This is the basic fact represented in the diagram at Stage 1. As sound waves and light waves they are capable of being sensed or received by a listener, and the listener who receives them is represented, with respect to what he does as a listener, in Stages 2, 3 and 4. At Stage 5 the listener becomes a speaker, or responder of some sort, and then the whole process, as diagramed, runs itself through again. Not quite in the same way, of course, and possibly very differently indeed, in consequence of the self-reflexive feedback—or, more aptly, feedback-and-forth—represented by the unending loop threading through the diagram.

What is produced when words are spoken at Stage 5, and what is transmitted at Stage 1, is a kind of code. It has something in common with Morse code, flag signals, or traffic lights, since it is made up of discrete units arranged according to rules. The code we call the English language, or so-called standard American speech, is considerably more elaborate, however, than flag signals or traffic lights, or even Morse code, and it provides for the transmission of a considerably greater variety and amount of information. For essentially the same reasons, of course, it allows for a relatively greater amount of disagreement between senders and receivers as to the meanings of the messages being transmitted. The meaning of a message is to be found, not in the words or other code signals that are transmitted, but in the sender and the receiver—and there is hardly any other fact concerning this entire process more significant than the fact that there is always a difference between the meaning of a message to be found in the sender and the meaning of the same message to be discovered in the receiver. This difference, of course, is often too slight to make any difference but occasionally it is so great as to be disastrous if not properly allowed for.

The outstanding implication of this fact, from a practical point of view, is that for effective communication to occur between speaker and listener there must be adequate feedback from listener to speaker. Monologues are hazardous. Moreover, the speaker must be properly receptive to this feedback. Finally, the listener has to be effectively receptive to the speaker's subsequent revisings, if any. The sender must send and resend; the receiver must take and retake.

This is an extremely brief summary of the conditions essential to the effective carrying on of ordinary conversation, group discussion, or any other form of the common but incredibly fateful process of people talking with one another. In *How to Talk with People* (Harper & Brothers, 1951), Irving Lee reports the observations he made as a by-sitter in two hundred meetings of boards and committees, and the major types of trouble that he found people having in trying to talk with each other all reflect in one way or another some sort of "jamming" of the feedback. People seem to be far more powerfully driven to talk at each other than to listen to each other, and when they do listen the kind of feedback they give the speaker—and the kind of reaction the speaker makes, in turn, to this feedback—appears distressingly often to be self-defensive and generally competitive, or insincere and thus misleading, rather than clarifying, honest, and co-operative.

To be highlighted in this connection is the strangely

underestimated fact that listeners can and frequently do feel gravely threatened by speakers. No one has yet presented a wholly satisfactory explanation—and doubtless there can be no simple explanation—of this curious relationship that so often develops between speakers and their listeners. The followers of Freud, Carl Rogers, and many other psychotherapists are wise in their ways of dealing with the problem of threat in its clinical forms, but as yet certainly no one has devised a foolproof way of enabling the run of people to deal with their feelings of being threatened by each other as speakers.

It would appear to be a useful notion, meanwhile, that as listeners we might minimize our feelings of being threatened by maintaining the clearest possible awareness of our own projecting. It helps also to do whatever might be feasible to check with the speaker in order to determine whether any such feelings as we may have at any time are justified, so far, at least, as the speaker's intentions are concerned. Within limits, we can as speakers reduce our listeners' feelings of being threatened simply by being alert to any possible manifestations of such feelings on their part, and by providing reassurances when they are called for, even if they are not asked for.

What makes this problem so intriguing is that as a matter of objective fact nothing passes from speaker to listener except air waves and light waves and, as such, as manifestations of physical force, they are impressively weak! Viewed mechanically, the sheer physical effects they sometimes produce are not obviously credible. These really feeble waves commonly disturb the cardiovascular system, endocrine glands, autonomic nervous system, skeletal musculature, even the digestive system of the listener, with effects ranging all the way from increased heart rate and blanching of the skin to regurgitation and even loss of consciousness. It appears beyond dispute that on occasion death itself has been a consequence of the reception of verbal messages. Meanwhile nothing except the gentlest of vibrations in the air and perfectly harmless reflections of light passes between speaker and listener—even when the speaker shouts, trembles, and jumps up and down quite violently. An effective awareness of this should go far to make listeners less fearful and speakers less confident of the threatening powers of words, particularly snarled or shouted words, as such.

These few remarks can only suggest the full range of events at Stage 1 and their intriguing consequences; our more immediate concern is with the goings-on at Stage 5. And what we shall observe at Stage 5 that is of particular interest to us just now are the things that can and often do go wrong in the overt act of speech. One of the major reasons why our attention is drawn to these misfirings of the speech mechanism is that an understanding of them, and their conditions and effects, helps considerably to make clear certain of the fundamental requirements of effective communication. To study the disorders of speech is to train a microscope, as it were, full upon certain essentials of normally ordered speech.

In its common usages the term "speech defect" is so interpreted as to warrant the estimate that 5 to 10 per cent of us have defective speech. What is meant by this, with reference to actual cases, falls under a number of more or less standard headings. In general terms, speech disorders in the textbook sense are classifiable as voice disorders, misarticulation of speech sounds, stuttering (a synonym for stuttering is stammering), and the aphasias or dysphasias.

Among the voice disorders the most serious is the complete or substantial loss of the physical ability to vocalize. As an example, cancer of the larynx, or voice box, is commonly treated by means of surgical removal of the larynx, leaving the patient without vocal cords. Such a patient may in these days attend a speech clinic and be taught to swallow air part way down into the esophagus and expel it as a belch which, when properly articulated, makes for serviceable and not unpleasant speech. The occasional patient for whom the surgical result does not permit this may use the modern artificial larynx, a sort of electrically driven buzzer. By holding this against his throat and articulating the "buzzing" sound as he would his own vocal tones, he may produce quite intelligible speech. The main purpose of selecting these examples is to make the point that even for some of the most serious vocal disabilities, there are remedial measures by means of which vocal communication may be restored. Most of the other voice disorders involve distortions of vocal quality, such as nasality, harshness, or breathiness, and as a rule these are clearly less serious. In most cases they do not gravely impair communication, and it is to be said in addition that improvement is generally to be expected from instruction to be had in present-day speech clinics.

This does not begin to exhaust the subject of voice disorders, but it is to be appreciated that exhaustive discussion of voice and speech impairments is not one of the purposes of this book. It is our purpose to indicate in a general way the nature of the problems in communication that can and sometimes do arise in the moment of actual utterance. It is to be expected that most readers will conclude that, by and large, these problems are not as serious in their effects on communication as are those we have considered in examining Stage 4.

It remains to be noted that while disorders of speech and voice are usually found in the absence of any significant physical "causes," they may be associated with—and may be fundamentally due to—such impairments as hearing loss or deafness, mental retardation, cleft palate, cerebral palsy, muscular paralysis, or brain damage. About three-fourths of the cerebral palsied have speech that is affected by the fact that the muscles used in breathing and in producing speech sounds do not function normally. In most of these cases speech is more or less intelligible, and in the majority improvement can be achieved through speech therapy. Important advances have been made in recent years in audiology, the science and craft that is concerned with the measurement of hearing, the use of hearing aids, lip reading and speech training for the deaf and hard of hearing, so that individuals whose speech problems are associated with hearing deficiencies have brighter futures than they used to have. The speech pathologists, and the dental and surgical specialists with whom they co-operate in teamwork fashion, are making exciting progress in their efforts to deal with the problems of speech and voice which center around cleft palate and cleft lip. Other speech pathologists, teaming up with neurologists and psychologists particularly, are having good hunting in their exploration of better ways to help the patients whose brain injuries affect their ability to understand and to use language. We call the difficulties of these patients aphasia or, more precisely, the dysphasias.

When we have run through this inventory, however, we have covered a small proportion, certainly not more than 20 per cent, and probably not over 15 per cent, of the speech handicapped persons who are served in speech clinics and in the ever-growing number of speech-correction programs in the elementary and high schools of the nation. The remaining 80 to 85 per cent of the eight to sixteen million persons with speech problems in the United States, as they are identified by professional speech correction workers, have speech and voice disorders that are not due, so far as can be demonstrated, to any physical or organic impairment. Worth-while improvement, often complete or practically so, can be brought about in these cases. They are those who do not form all of the speech sounds properly, or they have voice quality characteristics that are noticeably different from those of most speakers, or they stutter.

Approximately a million persons in the United States, quite possibly a few more than that, stutter more or less severely. A great deal of scientific research on stuttering has been done in the past twenty-five years or so, and the findings have indicated mainly that it develops as a rule in essentially normal youngsters, usually around the age of three years. Their speech problems appear to be brought on mainly, though unintentionally, by parents who are not dramatically different from other parents, but who tend, on the average, to be rather more perfectionistic than most mothers and fathers, especially about the smoothness or fluency of their children's speech. And at the age of three normal children do not speak very smoothly, the average of them repeating a sound or word or phrase forty-five times or so every thousand running words, so that a parent with sufficiently high standards can find much to be concerned about in the speech of practically any three-year-old, even though the great majority of parents and other people would not. This essential circumstance of a youngster speak-

ing normally but not fluently enough to suit a comparatively perfectionistic parent, with consequent self-consciousness and uneasiness and tense striving on the part of the
child to regain the approval of the increasingly concerned
parent—this essential circumstance is to be found in a
great variety of specific settings involving individuals who
are by no means monotonously similar. It is found to
have an impressive variety of consequences, as well, so that,
comprehensively considered, the problem of stuttering is far
more complex than most people would be prepared to believe. Speech clinicians are learning, however, to deal with
it more and more successfully, and, although results are
best with young children, even adults who stutter severely
have good reason to be much more than faintly hopeful
these days.

As to the vast majority of individuals who have faults of
articulation and voice, their disturbed speech is, even to a
greater degree than stuttering, subject to correction or improvement. Moreover, most persons with speech difficulties,
including a large proportion of those whose disordered
speech is importantly associated with organic impairment,
have speech that can be understood either with little difficulty or as readily as most other speech is understood.

There are, then, two main statements to be made about
these speech impairments, so far as they relate to our present
objectives. The one is that they disturb communication to
the extent that they distort the messages being transmitted;
the other is that they do not disturb communication nearly
as much as do our faulty modes of listening. As has just been
pointed out, the speech of the great majority of the speech
handicapped is quite intelligible. It is, or nearly always
would be, relatively adequate for communicative purposes

were it not for the strong tendency we have as listeners to pay so much attention to how speakers sound that we lose out on what they say.

Most speakers who lisp, substituting the soft *th* sound for the *s* as in Mithithippi, can be understood very well by anyone who does not insist on the *s*'s to which he is accustomed. There is nothing especially unintelligible about nasal voices or loud or shrill ones. Nearly all of the speech of most stutterers is clearly understandable. Our reaction to so-called defective speech—especially after we have classified it as "defective" in any specific case—is chiefly an aesthetic matter, when it is not one simply of custom and habit. As listeners we are inclined to be quite fussy about things that are nonessential so far as communication is concerned. We are all too often more finicky about the sheer sound of the message than we are about its clarity, validity, and factual significance. With a like attitude toward money we would be attracted or repelled by the fact that it is green or crinkly while remaining oblivious to the shoes or cucumbers for which we could or could not exchange it.

To the extent that disorders of speech and voice do make the speaker difficult to understand, they should, of course, in the interests of communication, be modified so far as possible. Anyone who has such a problem should be aware of the fact that there are professional speech pathologists and speech correctionists these days. They are trained in the universities, but, of course, the laws and customs governing such things being what they are, it is well to inquire of the offices of the American Speech and Hearing Association (a permanent usable address is Speech Correction Fund, c/o The National Society for Crippled Children and Adults, 11 South LaSalle Street, Chicago, Illinois) in order to locate speech correction workers in particular localities and to determine whether they hold either basic or advanced clinical certification— not membership only—in the American Speech and Hearing Association. If they do not, the burden of proof is necessarily on them to show that they are, in fact, professionally qualified, since the Association is the nationally recognized organization of professional workers in this field, and its clinical certification requirements constitute a generally agreed-upon set of standards for those who minister professionally to children and adults with speech and voice disorders.

For the general run of people who do not have faulty speech in a clinical sense there are two practical suggestions to be offered concerning speech improvement: Try to speak up loudly enough to be heard—and check now and then to see that you have been—and try to speak plainly, not jamming your words together or leaving off final sounds, for example. Be conscious always of the fact that there is someone listening, trying to hear you, and trying to understand you. Speech is not just to be sent—it is also to be received. Speak plainly. Speak up. And check up. If you have no well-developed speech disorders, you may be able to make use of these common-sense suggestions. To reduce advice about these matters, however, to such simple slogans is something to be done only with insistent warnings of the hazards involved in trying to swallow these capsules of exhortation. They may not go down, or if they do they may come back up. They will seldom be sufficient. Anyone who has a definite speech or voice problem, or a strong desire to improve his speech, should by all means consult personally a qualified speech pathologist.

Indeed, if you have what passes for a speech disorder, even though your speech is understandable, so long as our culture places a high premium on aesthetically pleasant and phonetically conventional speech, you might as well not be too stubborn about falling into line. If you have no good reasons for retaining the impairment, and if it can be corrected, you would seem to be well advised to undergo the training necessary to reduce or remove it. If you are going to insist on opposing the dominant tastes or convictions of society, you can doubtless find other far more significant grounds on which to take a stand and fight it out. Indeed, the positive gains resulting from the elimination of shortcomings in speech and the cultivation of more and more clear, pleasing, and generally effective speech are almost always substantial far beyond expectation. To be human at all is to speak, however poorly, and to be human at best is to speak exceptionally well.

This is by no means intended to imply that we should not attempt to improve our ways of listening to speech, including speech that is faulty. It seems reasonable to contend that it is far more important to evaluate effectively what a speaker says than it is to notice the dialect, diction, inflection, rhythm pattern, or voice quality he uses in saying it. And this brings us back to the second main observation to be made with reference to speech disorders so far as our major objectives in this book are concerned. The chief importance of these faults does not lie in the fact that they distort the messages to be communicated, because most of them do not distort the messages very much, if at all, but it lies rather in the fact that so many listeners permit themselves to be unduly distracted by them. The fundamental consideration is that by and large we are not good listeners.

It is hardly fair to say that training in effective listening is entirely neglected in our schools and colleges. It would be misleading, however, to make out that anything very systematic or significant is done about it except by a few unusual teachers, who necessarily labor in the main without as much knowledge as they would like to have and with something less than fully developed procedures. In general, it is probably true that what is done for the most part in teaching students how to listen is rather similar to what is done in teaching them how to read. There is one important difference, of course: The rate of reading is under the control of the reader, whereas the listener can "receive" words only at the rate at which the speaker "sends" them. The similarity lies largely in the fact that emphasis is placed, in currently accepted methods of training with respect to both reading and listening, on paying attention to the "message," separating the more important from the less important details, and remembering or retaining what is taken in. The ways in which reading or listening "comprehension" is measured indicate that those who devise the measurements mean by "comprehension" primarily the ability to recall immediately, or at some later time, a sampling of what the writer or speaker has said. Seldom does the "comprehension" that is measured have anything to do with the ability to weigh or evaluate or improve upon what is recalled. Practically never is it concerned with what the individual *does* as a consequence of having read or heard something. It is easier, of course, to gauge "comprehension" in terms of simple recall, and yet this plays its own part, small or large, in fostering a kind of listening, or reading, that emphasizes the acceptance and retention rather than the critical and creative evaluation of what is received. It does not encourage one to develop the implications of the message nor to extend and refine it. It encourages the student to listen the way a tape recorder "listens"—and consequently to speak the way a tape recorder "speaks." It is as though the instructor were to talk "into his students" on Mondays and Wednesdays and to "play them back" in a quiz every Friday.

A peculiarly unsuspected or disregarded fact is that our most serious speech disorders are more often than not found in persons whose voices are strong and clear, whose sounds are plainly enunciated, and whose speech moves on its forward course as gaily as a willow stick in a meadow brook— but whose messages are faulty. What such a speaker says may distress or confuse or deprave those who hear it, including the speaker himself—if not, indeed, the speaker most of all. The hazards we create for ourselves as speakers and listeners by lisping or stuttering are as flea bites compared to the seven-year itches we bring upon our unserene selves by speaking without due regard to the requirements of clarity, validity, and a clear consciousness of abstracting and projecting. A sane and neighborly lisper is ever so greatly to be preferred to a silver-tongued paranoid.

It is at Stage 5 that the processes which go on at Stage 4 become vocal. What are, at Stage 4, disorders of evaluation and of symbolic formulation become, at Stage 5, disorders of speech in its overt, hearable, public forms. At this stage, then, oversimplification and overgeneralization, misidentification and unconscious projection, the joining of the unrelated, the disengaging of the unified, the communing with verbal spirits, and, in general, the confusing and disorderly intermingling of the levels of abstraction—of what can be seen with what can be inferred, of what can be felt with what can be said, the general misidentifying of abstractions with what they may be abstractions of—at Stage 5 this unholy flock takes wing. Loosed upon the world, not from one mouth flung wide but from one multiplied by hundreds of millions, they form around the earth a rind of whirring.

The statistic that 5 to 10 per cent of us have speech disorders is to be reread and relegated to its own narrow niche of meaning in consideration of this more comprehensive appraisal of the range within which speech may be found to be a less than trustworthy vehicle of communication.

A listener so oriented as to find these observations congenial is quite likely to react with a functional rather than a fussy attitude toward such incidental characteristics of speech as inflectional patterns, modes of speech sound articulation, and patterns of fluency, as well as idiosyncrasies of word choice and pronunciation. He is likely to be a listener who is willing to reach out for understanding and to co-operate quite energetically if need be with the "source of the message," even when the source is near to baffling in its tendency to render the message obscure or dull or unintelligible, provided the message turns out to be "either true or delightful."

We sin as speakers and as listeners we repent—if ever we do repent at all. For our sins as speakers we all too often do not suspect, or we claim them with proud innocence as virtues. The air waves that we unthinkingly fashion in our throats we blow all too devotedly into the ears of our fellows, and their little auditory bones and membranes quiver our messages onto the nerve filaments which so unhesitatingly speed them home to a consciousness that is seldom sufficiently conscious of itself to make for listening that is keenly discerning and just and creative.

And as listeners unto our own sounding selves we are in like ways affected—as by a concert of our own echoes.

All these remarkable events seem to take place quite as

though they were happening to us rather than to be of our own designed or witless doing—and as clear a perception of this illusion as we might with all our ingenuity achieve prepares us to understand the limitations of our capacity for knowing truth and being wise.

. . . all we gain from wonder by wonder is increased.

CHAPTER SEVENTEEN

Gentle Bravery

✳ It has been our purpose in this book to explore the possibilities of method for bringing about a closer union of clear thinking and good will. Since the most effective procedure man has developed for dealing with his problems appears to be the scientific method, it has seemed sensible to consider whether this might be adapted to our purpose. We have been handicapped in pursuing this question, however, because nearly all of us have absorbed from our culture a strong bias to the effect that science is used and can only be used within a relatively small part of our lives. Doubtless most of us assume that, strictly speaking, scientific activities are carried on only in laboratories or research organizations, and that the individual, wending his private journey each day from sleep to slumber, cannot be scientific in any vital sense in relating himself to his world or to his fellows.

It would seem that few of us, however, are completely free of the haunting hope that the best we have learned to do we may yet learn to do more often and more extensively. Each new success, however trivial, of man as scientist must necessarily inspire, however vaguely, man as citizen. And when, to our restrained terror, we discover that we have learned to shatter cities with our atomic thoughts, there is awakened deep within our dim consciousness a writhing and insistent wish to make more kindly and creative the lives that we can only otherwise, with our new cleverness, mangle and beat dead.

The new world, if there is to be one, must indeed be brave. And it must be gentle too. Brave enough to leave home like a strong-hearted lad, to turn away from all there is in man's traditions that make it hard for men to be gentle with one another. If men can be as brave as that they will surely then become gentle enough to live together even with their atomic thoughts, and to withstand too the grandest and most demanding of the dreams they have yet to know.

Whatever else may be involved in the design for gentle bravery such as this, it must include the freedom and the will to inquire, to ask questions with a clear intention to seek their answers through disciplined perception. This surely is a part of the method of science that need not be confined to laboratories. It is a part of the method that we and all our children may learn and cultivate by nearly constant practice in all our circumstances.

The new world bravery must thrive too on order and honesty in perceiving, on seeing that is as undistorted by believing and wishing, by loving and hating and discouragement, as it may be. This as well is a part of scientific method that we may use, nearly always and everywhere, as adroitly or as crudely as our aptitudes and situations will allow.

The brave, moreover, may not refrain from the frank reporting of the observations they make in their efforts to answer the questions they ask. Yet if they are gentle they do not give their accounts harshly or with arrogance, insensitive to the inner feelings of those who have yet to see what meanwhile can be only words to them. And this is a marriage of compassion and forthrightness that may be solemnized by any one of us, clothed only in the vestments of humanity.

Into the design for gentle bravery there is also to be woven a dependable tendency to draw from one's honestly reported observations only such hypotheses or statements of relationship, predictions or other conclusions as reasoned inference will allow—and these only with the firm intention to subject them to the test of further observation, and to seek honest answers to the further questions they imply. Such discipline of reason need by no means be disavowed by all save those who pursue truth with cyclotrons and microscopes.

We may all and everywhere draw prudent conclusions as best we can from our honest reports of observations that we have made with care in trying to answer the clearest questions we have been able to fashion. And always we may go on to the further adventures of inquiry to which our ever-new conclusions unfailingly lead us, if only we welcome adventure.

This, without accessories of technical and theoretical refinement, would appear to be the method that we recognize as scientific. It turns out to be, in main essentials, a mode of symbolization—a manner of speaking. It is a way of speaking with an alert readiness to answer what we can, and to acknowledge what we cannot answer, to the question, "What do you mean?" It is a manner of saying words with a sensitivity to the fact that what we mean by them is to be demonstrated not alone "in other words," whether more abstract or less so, but also on the level of not-words, the level of our perceptions and our feelings and our actions and of the facts we have not seen but take to be perceivable. And if we are to appreciate our meanings on these levels, we must be in some measure aware of our meanings on the deeper level that lies beyond the reach of our senses, even when aided by our most sensitive instruments—the level on which we fashion the creations of our imaginations, our protons and our gremlins and our great movers, which we do not see, and yet without which we seem incapable of seeing anything we look at with a sense of understanding.

It is a manner of speaking that requires as well a readiness to make clear the grounds—and their boundaries—for contending that what we say is true or dependable or useful. Given such a manner of speaking, it is to be maintained only by habits of inquiry and observation that are unintimidated and responsible, and by methods of analyzing and evaluating the data of observation that are conducive to orderly and candid inference.

Those who reach well beyond these modest endeavors and objectives, meaning to make a profession of science, have need of great technical skill and theoretical sophistication. The farthest frontiers of science are extended by those who exercise a hardy disregard of possible immediate gains of material and practical sorts in devoting themselves to pure research, designed to further the continuing refinement of definitions and techniques and the unceasing revision of basic assumptions and theoretical systems. On these frontiers we may, should we be searching, come upon no end of lonely heroes to encourage—for the greatest good of all mankind.

For very few of us, however, is science a profession, nor will it ever be, and it is not our present purpose to consider how mean or glorious may be the way of the technical or philosophical specialist. We have been at pains to determine what it is that scientists do—while they are behaving scientifically—that all men everywhere might do, each with such aptitude as he may possess or acquire, and for his own great or trivial purposes in his own way. It would appear that there is much that is scientific that we all might do, however crudely or well, in dealing with our daily circumstances. But we seldom do these things. Go where we will, we observe our fellows alertly defending their beliefs against the encroachments of fact, cherishing as natural and right their locally conditioned attitudes and customs, and declining to question their settled habits and convictions. And each of us tends to be in these respects much like our fellows.

Even from our campuses come thousands every spring who say that in the halls of higher learning they have been taught to believe that science tells us what and how but never why nor whether. And so they go through life, as nearly all men do, asking their whys and whethers with an air of thoughtlessness, not quite expecting answers, save those which in their tender years they learned so trustingly and well. Indeed, by other answers they appear—each one of us appears in some degree—to be dismayed. It is when asking what and how that we reveal such shrewdness as we might have gained from schooling. But even much of what we say about what is, and how it is things work the ways they do, we seem to say without wonder, as though it were enough to make it so to cite a book, or to recall a teacher's name, or quote a transient headline.

Meanwhile, many or all of our whys and whethers could, with little trouble, be caught a moment on the tongue and inspected for the flaws of vagueness and illusion before we give them vocal wing. And many an answer to them could be checked for fact and implication quite as readily as are the answers to our hows and whats. The obligation to speak as clearly and dependably as possible, and to acknowledge as fully as we can the vagaries of our projections, may not be lightly disregarded, once accepted. When the only defensible answer to "What do you mean?" is "I don't know," we may not graciously claim that this answer need not be given. And when, to any question that cannot be answered with direct or indirect reference to observable facts, we give a confident answer nonetheless, our more thoughtful listeners can hardly take such audacity to be a fair reaction to the question, "How do you know?"

There is a code of honor inherent in scientific behavior that we may set aside in any circumstance only at the risk of dishonor. We would seem quite clearly to take that risk whenever we contend that there are matters—by whatever grand names we call them, such as "ethics" or "morals" or "values"—about which we may speak without regard to this code.

It must surely be a moderate supposition that the wonders we have so far accomplished by being scientific about the world in which we live, we can duplicate and multiply by employing, with gentle bravery, the scientific method to investigate ourselves and our cultures—and to test the limits of our possibilities for creative change. While man has always been both the sculptor and the stone, yet we may come to discover that so far he has been more the stone and less the sculptor than he need have been.

If we are to test this possibility and explore its implications, we can probably not do better than to focus the method of scientific investigation and experiment on what we seem to try to mean by our "unconscious." We may view "the unconscious," especially for this purpose, as meaning not mainly—certainly not only—what we have been motivated to forget or repress, but most especially what we have come to take for granted. The sense of this was caught up adroitly in Ruth Benedict's arresting reflection that it would hardly have been fish that would have discovered water. So we may suppose that, as in "the unconscious" of fish there are mainly water and swimming, and in that of birds the air and flying, so in "the unconscious" of man surely there are chiefly symbols and symbolizing.

By symbols in this context we must mean not only words and other codes but also the grand range of our symbolic creations from crucifixes to crowns, from pyramids to skyscrapers. Nor may we disregard the dreams and sentiments, the values and ideals, the knowledge and the whimsy that we should never have except for symbols. We must consider as well the communicating that we do with symbols, and so too all those forms of human association and organization that communicating fosters, and which in turn make communication among human beings something new under the evolutionary sun. Contemplating these things, we are prompted necessarily to ponder a crucial difference between men and such other creatures as the fishes and the birds.

The difference that enables man to blink his tortuous way, however slowly, out of the dark cocoon of his unconscious, whereas the birds and the fishes remain, so we must think, forever unknowing of the air and the sea—the difference would appear to reside in a characteristic peculiar to symbols. A symbol is any sign, natural like a clap of thunder or man-made like a flag or word, into which men project the meanings they themselves design, or borrow from each other. And symbols function self-reflexively. This means that there are symbols of symbols, languages about language, words about words about words. And as man long ago began, ever so inadvertently, to talk about the talking that he did, he started his slow fumbling toward the far pinpoint of light that promises ever more surely to be the great sun of his self-awareness.

Certainly as we succeed bit by small bit in transforming our unconscious into a growing sense of consciousness, we can hardly come to believe otherwise but that we make our way in this adventure by the creation and the contemplation of our symbols. We proceed most adroitly by making comments about the comments we have made. And we make our greatest gains as we build up, layer upon layer, the more and more adequate language which enables us to comment more and more incisively upon our crucial bodily process of symbolization and its products, and their effects by which, alone, we are distinguished from the creatures that only swim or fly.

And we have, perhaps quite early in the human day, gained access to the view that man and his world are fashioned the one by the other to an important degree and unceasingly. The world that we may understand, and to which we may relate ourselves more or less well, is in large measure our own and our forebears' creation. Certainly this is true for those aspects of it that matter most to us as human beings. And we, in our own turn, are bound to use, in our endeavor to understand that world, the very beliefs and modes of conduct which are part and parcel of it, and which we receive as a heritage from it.

The words to which we are accustomed mostly fail to achieve for us quite what we intend to say about this complex situation. In one of her happier moments of contemplation, Gertrude Stein, in *Wars I Have Seen,* succeeded in weaving together the words with which we seek to reclaim the past and those other words by which we strive to capture the present—she succeeded in weaving these together into a verbal pattern that fit with new gracefulness the inconstant contours of experience. She managed to make peculiarly clear that what for each of us is largely present in the present is the past. To hazard a further recasting of her apparent implications, our lives are not simply remembered and forgotten, savored in the present or recalled from times gone, but rather the time in which we live is one for which we must make a new name, for it is neither the past nor the present but rather a sort of then-now. And what we should nearly always want to mean by "then-now" would be gravely misrepresented by referring to it as either the past or the present. Beyond these observations, of course, lies the unwanted fact that the words we need in order to express what we seem never able to say with "the future" are quite evidently still to be fashioned.

One who knew Alfred Korzybski must never have wholly forgotten the implications of the particular ways in which he often observed that there is no time in nature, there are times only. This generalization must have been what Gertrude Stein was trying to snare with the words with which she wrote *Wars I Have Seen.* It is something, however, that we mainly disregard in our common speech, so that

we talk about sequences in a most bewildering fashion, referring glibly to what we have done and have had and will
do and are having, as though we were stringing hard beads
of history on a stiff wire of time—rather than adding now
and then, as of course we do, a new carrot and a little water
to the age-old and ever-blending stew of human experience.

But it is not only times that our common language fits
so poorly. The words with which we speak of you and me
and I and we and they seem to make peace and good will
more difficult to come by than should otherwise be so. And
yet there is, of course, a wisdom that we have beyond these
pronouns by which we know how inept we nearly always
are in using them.

A part of the underlining needed for these statements is
provided in a charming way by a story, the origin of which
I do not know, that was told me one day by Major Charles
Estes. It is about an old Indian woman who came down
from her home far up in the Andes into a tiny village in
Peru, and, finding herself beside a house with a window
of glass that arrested her attention, she ran her wrinkled
fingers feelingly over the pane, and then her hands came to
rest as she noticed children playing inside the house. Seeing
her kindly face peering at them through the glass, they in-
vited her in. She stayed awhile, surrounded by their many
laughing voices and friendly faces, and it was plain that she
enjoyed being with them. When, rested and refreshed in
spirit, she took her leave she spoke to them some Indian
words they could not understand, although her sounds they
could re-form and remember. After she had gone the
children repeated the sounds of her words to a neighbor
who was able to make out a translation of them—and the

words she had spoken to the children had been: "I like me when I am with you."

These are common words with which, lacking the gentle Indian woman's wisdom of feeling, we symbolically disfigure our lives. We know, in spite of our words, that there is no I alone and isolated in nature, nor any separate you, and that what we sometimes say so well with "we" we all too often spoil by what we add with "they." There is hardly any other condition of man more unnerving than loneliness, and so it is that there are hardly any other words in our language that we may use carelessly with more despairing effects than "I" and "you." The me for whom the bell tolls is not indeed an island unto itself.

The barriers of feeling that we innocently raise—through our glib use of singular pronouns—between our individual selves and those others whom we long to gladden and enjoy, these are as miniatures compared with the huge semantic Chinese Walls which men construct throughout the world in their exertions to protect Us from Them. In the world that we have made They are real and so are We, as real as the engines of destruction we have invented and the vehicles of flight we have built to deliver them upon One Another. But in the non-verbal bowels of our wisdom we know that there is something still more substantial than these, which we can speak about by using "we" and "us" only if we do not oppose these words to "they" and "them."

The evils of our ways we commit very nearly altogether in the names of great categories and verbal fictions. The killing we chance to do while waving the pennant of I is as nothing compared to the grand slaughters we achieve with sorrowing pride under the banner of We. And those whom

We destroy are ones of us, as we are ones of Them by whom we are destroyed.

These things we must sometimes have learned, and may always learn anew, by asking of our talking selves quite simply what we mean and how we know that what we say is so. For by these questions we persuade ourselves to test our high abstractions against the litmus of sensation, and to compare our private perceptions with those of our fellows, being ever careful to subtract the believing that is seeing from the seeing to be believed.

And when we have conscientiously tested and compared, it is, even so, to be remembered that whatever the words we utter, they can never be about reality except as we have privately filtered through the mesh of our nervous tissues whatever reality might be. Whatever it might be meanwhile we can never know undoubtingly, for, as we have considered, there is for all of us a point beyond which, even with our most powerful lenses, and amplifiers and seismographs, we are blind, we do not hear, and we are numb in a realm where for us nothing sweet or sour or fragrant is. But that which we cannot know we can picture and construct symbolically in ways congenial to the knowledge we possess. And knowing that is what we do, our freedom to do it seems immense, for it is not easy, if possible at all, to believe that there are firm limits to the creativeness we might achieve with symbols.

This freedom that is ours to fashion and refashion the worlds within us is the grandest freedom of the human spirit. It is the ever-flowing spring of myth with all its proud and plaintive intimations of man's ends and purposes. From it is ever born the wonder that is poetry and song. Out of it arises the strangely enduring serenity of those utopias toward which men in their mortal striving goad themselves, and those they cherish in unvisited foreverwheres. And from this same freedom men have forged, as well, the way of science, the modern witchery, a method of contriving methods with which to change the shape of things that are and might be. Possessed of it, in awed astonishment, we are destined to weigh ever more decisively its mounting threat against its fair promise of worlds more wonderful by far than any man has known in fact or longing.

Acknowledgments

Permission granted by the organizations and individuals concerned to quote from the following sources is gratefully acknowledged:

Scientific American: "Seeing Light and Color," by Ralph M. Evans, *Scientific American,* August, 1949.

Psychiatry, William Alanson White Memorial Foundation: "Psychiatry of Enduring Peace and Social Progress," by G. B. Chisholm, *Psychiatry,* Volume 9, Number 1, February, 1946, 3-20.

Quarterly Journal of Speech, Speech Association of America: "The Spoken Word and the Great Unsaid," by Wendell Johnson, Volume 37, December, 1951, 419-429.

Psychological Monographs, American Psychological Association: "A Statistical and Comparative Analysis of Individual Written Language Samples," by John W. Chotlos, *Psychological Monographs,* Volume 56, Number 2, 1944, 77-111.

Major Charles T. Estes: personal communication to the author.

ETC.: A Review of General Semantics, International Society for General Semantics: "Do You Know How to Listen?" by Wendell Johnson, *ETC.: A Review of General Semantics,* August, 1949.

Twilight of the Gladiators, by Frank Heller, translated by Llewellyn Jones, published, 1944, by G. P. Putnam's Sons.

Index

213

For a free catalogue of books on semantics
and improving communication, write:
INTERNATIONAL SOCIETY FOR GENERAL SEMANTICS
P.O. Box 2469   San Francisco, California 94126